Treasures in Heaven

William Ayles, D.D.

Nancy & Barry,

May your
Treasures in
Heaven
ovERFLOW!
Blessings,
Bill

Treasures in Heaven

William Ayles, D.D.

How treasures in Heaven inspire us on this Earth and bless us on the new Earth

TIMELINE INTERNATIONAL is a research group dedicated to the methodical exploration and dynamic presentation of the inherent accuracy and integrity of the Word of God.

ISBN: 978-0-9978863-9-9

Dedication

This book is dedicated to my father and mother.

I couldn't have asked for better parents.

The Scriptures

The Scriptures in this book are taken from many versions of the Bible. This will give you a greater perspective.

Proverbs

My son, if you accept my words and store up my commands within you, turning your ear to wisdom and applying your heart to understanding—indeed, if you call out for insight and cry aloud for understanding, and if you look for it as for silver and search for it as for hidden treasure, then you will understand the fear [reverence] of the Lord and find the knowledge of God. (Prov. 2:1–5)

Contents

Acknowledgments... i

Author's Note... 3

Prologue... 5

ACT ONE 11

1 Eternal Victory 13

2 Treasures: Our Invitation 31

3 Treasures: Eternal Crowns 45

ACT TWO 63

4 The Appearance of Our King 65

5 Treasures: The *Bema* 79

6 Treasures: Our Inheritance........................... 89

ACT THREE... 99

7 In the Beginning...101

8 Treasure: The Mystery................................ 119

9 Treasure in Earthen Vessels 133

Epilogue: The Chronology of Prophecy..........163

Revelation: Timeline...................................... 227

The End: Creation, Theory
 and Prophecy.. 229

The 40th Psalm...251

The Photographs.. 255

Endnotes 257

Acknowledgments

I developed this manuscript with the intention of having focus groups along the way so I could receive real-time feedback on the text. I wanted this to be a partnership. It is with the deepest appreciation that I extend my heartfelt thanks to those who worked in harmony with me. Lynn Moirs, who was with me start to finish, exhibited a tireless passion for prophecy, yielding input critical to the book's development and completion. Evelyne Castiglione, Suzanne Edgaro, and Charles Floyd all invited me into their homes, where we broke bread, talked about the nature of Heaven's treasures, and affected the way the book presents. Dr. Arthur Rouner and I sat on his dock on Lake Ossipee in New Hampshire as he recalled the days when God answered his prayer. I quoted Dr. Rouner in Chapter 9 about his experience—and he gave his blessing upon that chapter. Danielle Schuster and I spent many hours on the phone, discussing God's Word and what it means to be a child of God in the context of treasures in Heaven. Aunt Grace and I had a conversation that ultimately resulted in the Author's Note. Lauren Salkin and Trudy Seagraves both provided meaningful insight at the Connecticut Authors and Publishers

Association meeting in Hartford, CT. Jake Smith and Jordan Smith, whom I met late in the development of this book, provided needed confirmation about the book's introduction. I would also like to thank my editors, Janice Cohen, Lauren Mary Homick, and Ruthie Slovik, who graciously provided their God-given talents early in the production of this five-year project. Leslie Brown and Rita Reali, my editors who reviewed the entire manuscript, both turned in a stellar performance, turning text into a book. It is said, "every author needs a good editor." I needed five! Dan Uitti, a gifted webmaster who is a joy to work with, created the finished product, readying the book for production. I wish to acknowledge my enduring appreciation for my dear friend, Vera, who always believes in me. I am forever thankful for my father, sister, and brother for understanding my never-ending agenda to write, and then write some more. To my mother I send out a very special thanks for her inspiration, which is ever with me. I am grateful for the followers of Christ who have gone before me, Christians who believed and taught the apostles' doctrine, and contributed to the body of scriptural knowledge from which I am privileged to draw. Finally, and most important, I'd like to thank God for changing my life—twice—and making this book possible.

Author's Note

W hat will it be like to stand before the throne of Christ?

From the Sermon on the Mount to the Book of Revelation, Christ prepared us for it.

This book is about being prepared—and inspired.

3

Prologue

Eternity...
This concept captured my attention a long time ago.
I had questions.
Why am I here?
What is my purpose?
What happens after I die?
How do I "get" to God?
How will I spend eternity?

These are the questions that kept me awake at night during my senior year in college (1980). The obvious problem with asking and pondering these questions is that you need answers—and answers did follow.

I attended an on-campus Bible study and I learned this: God is relevant.

I realized—and felt—what Jesus of Nazareth said: "Then you will know the truth, and the truth will set you free."[1]

I was set *free*.

Jesus Christ—the anointed One sent by God—handed me divine peace. He granted me access to His eternal kingdom. And He empowered me with a supernatural sign.

I was never the same. Thank God.

Within every one of us is the desire to be

fulfilled. Atheists, agnostics, and believers are all seeking fulfillment, but we all make radically different choices in life. In my case, in 1980, I knew, beyond all reasonable doubt, that my fulfillment would now be found searching the knowledge of God.

Exactly 20 years after Christ set me free, He intervened in my life again. He transformed me from the inside out, again. Christ placed a fork in my road. It was not natural. It was supernatural. I experienced six weeks of His intervention, and promptly moved out to a cottage by a lake and began writing.

I have been compelled to write about Him ever since. I'm not saying an angel sits on my shoulder, dictating what to write. It's about the cause behind the effect; it's the inspiration. That's why I wrote this book: It's His inspiration to look at our future life through His eyes, and to look at our lives now through His.

This book is about seeing our lives—and our future life—through His invitation: "store up for yourselves treasures in Heaven."[2]

With this invitation we are "asked" to answer relevant questions.

Why did Christ give us this invitation?

What are treasures in Heaven?

How do we store them up?

Throughout the entire New Testament, Christ the King revealed the glory of Heaven's treasures, and this is what He presented: To store up treasures in Heaven is to seize the moment in the "here and now," and it is to receive all that Heaven has to bestow in the "hereafter." He also revealed this: Storing up treasures is not about chasing after a pot of gold; it is about a transformation of the "eyes." Christ presented Heaven's treasures to transform what we see. If we step out the door and see treasures in Heaven, it is clear we have accepted His invitation.

Our eyes are designed to see the current moment in light of the future for good reason. Jesus Christ revealed that Earth is a staging area for all future events. Life in this world shall profoundly affect the hereafter. The hereafter speaks of a time when prophecies about the future shall be fulfilled. The ultimate fulfillment is a time when Jesus Christ, who currently reigns in Heaven, will reign as King on the new Earth, which is the eternal paradise. And the treasures we store up in Heaven (in this life), will be with us forever on the new Earth (in the next life).

That is the heart of this book. Grasp the moment. Love your future.

About This Book

The best way to invite you into this book is to first invite you into God's book: the Bible.

Contrary to popular belief, the Bible is not like a bad game of telephone, where prophets and apostles passed along information from one to another and the end result is a garbled transmission.

We are set free by truth, not confused nonsense.

"All Scripture is given by inspiration of God."[3] There is one author, God, who gave us sixty-six books in the Bible, and He did so through the prophets and apostles of His choosing. Our Creator speaks with one voice, but with different perspectives on identical subjects. Consider Matthew, Mark, Luke, and John. Why four Gospels? They speak to the same subject, only with different perspectives, so as to paint the fullness of the whole picture. God designed the whole Bible this way, different writers speaking to identical subjects, providing unique pieces of the divine puzzle. His revelation unfolds over time.

This book presents unique pieces of the divine puzzle, which paints the picture of Heaven's treasures. It ends with a presentation on creation itself. My best response to those who subscribe to science is this: subscribe to evidence.

Act One is about our lives now.

Chapter 1 addresses the New Covenant delivered by God's Son and answers the question that I had: How do you reach out to God?

Chapters 2 and 3 open Heaven's treasure chest, unveiling what Christ said about storing up treasures in Heaven.

Act Two is about our life in the future.

Chapter 4 declares our hope, heralding the prophecies of Christ's appearance in the sky, when He will harvest His kingdom from the

Earth to His throne.

Chapter 5 reveals what it will be like to stand before the throne of Christ.

Chapter 6 unveils the eternal inheritance.

Act Three opens a window into our past and reflects what that means in our present.

Chapter 7 goes back in time. It documents the war between God and Lucifer, and how, through Jesus, God would defeat Lucifer, destroy death, and thus open the door to an eternal kingdom for mankind.

Chapter 8 presents God's hidden wisdom, which is revealed to those who seek the Messiah, the Savior, Jesus Christ, the Son of God.

Chapter 9 is about the treasures within, being empowered by God with a supernatural sign.

The Epilogue puts Heaven's treasures into perspective by presenting the sequence of end-time events, including the creation of the new Earth.

All of this divine revelation about treasures was made known in the first century A.D. Yet, in the twenty-first century, how many of us can recall hearing about Heaven's treasures? Is it possible that this treasure of knowledge remains essentially a mystery?

Consider Christ's will. Seven times in the Book of Revelation He spoke to His churches about Heaven's treasures. In each case, He concluded by saying this: "He who has an ear, let him hear what the Spirit says to the churches."[4]

May we all have ears to hear.

Finally, a few months back, I had a dream. I heard a voice in my head that said, "What really matters?" Then I heard, "At the end of the day, how do you feel about that?"

At that moment, I heard a doorbell ring. I woke up, shot out of bed, and looked out the window. No one was there.

It was a wakeup call... Seize the day!

ACT ONE

1

Eternal Victory

For everyone born of God overcomes the
world. This is the victory that has overcome
the world, even our faith. Who is it that
overcomes the world? Only he who believes
that Jesus is the Son of God.
                        —The Apostle John (1 John 5:4, 5)

Recently, I was reading an interview
given by Bob Dylan (who embraced
Jesus as his Lord, and sang about
being "saved by the blood of the Lamb"5). Dylan
said, "I knew Jimi Hendrix. I knew Janis Joplin.
If they knew then what I know now, they'd still
be here."6

We lost Hendrix and Joplin much too soon.
Each didn't know what they didn't know.

That's just it: We don't know what we don't
know, and if what we don't know is the truth,
that's tragic.

That's where I was. Just give me the truth.
In 1980, it happened.

I learned that Christianity is the only major
faith in the world where you "arrive" (are saved)
by the work of someone else (Jesus Christ). He

brought the New Covenant (agreement) from His Father. At the Last Supper, Jesus said, "This cup is the new covenant in my blood, which is poured out for you" (Luke 22:20). The New Covenant is not about memorizing rules, but meeting Jesus—receiving eternal life and living in that divine light.

The New Covenant

Two thousand years ago, our Creator sent forth His Son, our Lord, to herald the dawn of a new era, the New Covenant, whereby all men would receive an opportunity to enter an eternal, spiritual kingdom. When His invitation is accepted, entrance into His kingdom is granted. The Son of God sealed this invitation with His own blood.

During the Crucifixion, the Son of God promised paradise to a man condemned to death, and thereby demonstrated the nature of the New Covenant. The crucified man recognized that Jesus was the Messiah and said, "'Jesus, remember me when you come into your kingdom.' Jesus answered him, 'I tell you the truth, today you will be with me in paradise'" (Luke 23:42, 43).

Christ justified a condemned man, acquitting him of all sin. In an instant, the condemned soul became the saved soul. On the Cross, condemnation was removed and replaced with God's righteousness. This is the New

Covenant Jesus brought from the Father. Eternal life would now be granted by grace (divine favor) from Heaven. The words of Jesus yielded a guarantee of life everlasting in paradise.

Christ was able to grant paradise to a man with a criminal record because Jesus' blood was the ransom paid by God: "The Son of Man did not come to be served, but to serve, and to give his life as a ransom for many" (Mark 10:45). When the blood of Christ is given in exchange for the life of a soul, that soul is liberated from mortality.

As recorded by the apostle Peter:

> You know that it was not with perishable things such as silver or gold that you were redeemed from the empty way of life, but with the precious blood of Christ, a lamb without blemish or defect. He was chosen before the creation of the world, but was revealed in these last times for your sake. (1 Peter 1:18–20)

Christ is the full payment for souls to cross the spiritual divide. Man cannot earn his freedom. The cleansing of sin is without charge. If any payment from mankind is necessary to attain salvation, then the blood of Christ was an insufficient ransom.

Through His Son, the heavenly Father "rescued us from the dominion of darkness and brought us into the kingdom of the Son he loves"

(Col. 1:13). God established the New Covenant, whereby the kingdom of Christ would be upon the Earth, filled with souls who accept His gift.

Once in the kingdom, the liberated soul is sanctified—set apart—for all eternity. No power of darkness can alter the fate of a soul reserved by God. "I [Christ] tell you the truth, whoever hears my word and believes him who sent me has eternal life and will not be condemned; he has crossed over from death to life" (John 5:24).

According to Christ's prophecy, once a soul crosses into eternal life, there is no slipping back. If eternal life is granted, it cannot be revoked. Instantaneously, the power of death over the soul is overcome. The condemned man who hung on the cross did not evolve into a state of righteousness. He was made to be that way. That's why he could be guaranteed paradise. Jesus apportioned grace on the Cross.

The apostle Paul wrote of this divine favor given by God: "It is by grace you have been saved, through faith—and this is not from yourselves, it is the gift of God—not by works, so that no one can boast" (Eph. 2:8, 9). "And if [salvation is] by grace, then it is no longer by works; if it were, grace would no longer be grace" (Rom. 11:6). Grace is no longer grace if the hand of man is necessary to push his own soul across the spiritual divide. It is through an act of God that immortality is attained. Through His love God gave us a redeemer:

When the kindness and love of God our

Savior appeared, he saved us, not because of the righteous things we had done, but because of his mercy. He saved us through the washing of rebirth and renewal by the Holy Spirit, whom he poured out on us generously through Jesus Christ our Savior. (Titus 3:4–6)

[Y]ou were washed, you were sanctified, you were justified in the name of the Lord Jesus Christ and by the Spirit of our God. (1 Cor. 6:11)

The Son of God opened the door to a spiritual kingdom, where entrance would not be earned but granted. To be "washed" is to be cleansed by the blood of the sacrifice, Jesus, the Lamb of God. To be "sanctified" is to be set apart for God (by the Holy Spirit within). To be "justified" is to be made just, or set free from unrighteousness.

The Creator made this possible by extending His hand to Earth through His Son, so that He could pour out His Spirit generously. Christ Himself elaborated upon the spiritual nature of His kingdom: "The kingdom of God does not come with your careful observation because the kingdom of God is within you" (Luke 17:20, 21). "The kingdom of God is not a matter of eating and drinking, but of righteousness, peace, and joy in the Holy Spirit" (Rom. 14:17). The true kingdom of God is not about carnal regulations that legislate food and drink, it is about the Holy

Spirit's spiritual presence and nature dwelling within the believer.

The true nature of our God, fully declared through Jesus, was first disclosed hundreds of years earlier by Moses, for he revealed the heart of our Creator. "The Lord, the Lord, the compassionate and gracious God, slow to anger, abounding in love and faithfulness, maintaining love to thousands, and forgiving wickedness, rebellion and sin" (Exod. 34:6, 7).

When Moses first wrote these words, he looked forward to the day that God would send a redeemer. He knew that through the promised Messiah, the heavenly Father would fully extend this compassion to Earth. However, neither Moses nor any other Old Testament prophet knew that one day all bloodlines could be born of God saved into the kingdom of Christ. In the Holy Land, Jesus introduced this New Covenant from God, explaining how to enter the kingdom:

> Now there was a man of the Pharisees named Nicodemus, a member of the Jewish ruling council. He came to Jesus at night and said, "Rabbi, we know you are a teacher who has come from God. For no one could perform the miraculous signs you are doing if God were not with him." In reply Jesus declared, "I tell you the truth, no one can see the kingdom of God unless he is born again." "How can a man be born when he is old?" Nicodemus asked. "Surely he cannot enter a second time into his mother's womb to be

born!" Jesus answered, "I tell you the truth, no one can enter the kingdom of God unless he is born of water and the Spirit. Flesh gives birth to flesh, but the Spirit gives birth to spirit. You should not be surprised at my saying, 'You must be born again.'" (John 3:1–7)

The flesh of man gives birth to the flesh of man. In contrast, God, who is Spirit, gives birth to an eternal, invisible, spiritual seed within man. This is the second birth of which Jesus and His apostles spoke.

As recorded in the writings of Peter, "You have been born again, not of perishable seed, but of imperishable, through the living and enduring word of God" (1 Peter 1:23). When the living and enduring word of God is believed, then the Creator creates spiritual seed within the soul that cannot perish.

This spiritual seed, which gives birth to eternal life, is "Christ in you, the hope of glory" (Col. 1:27).

Christ is not just seated at the right hand of God, His Spirit lives within you. The Spirit of "Christ in you" is both life in this world and the hope of future glory in the next. When the Spirit of Christ lives within, that spiritual seed will ultimately give birth to a new spiritual body.

No act of man can cause the spiritual seed of Christ to be removed or destroyed. The soul that is born again of Spirit cannot be unborn. The indwelling Spirit is Heaven's spiritual seal upon the soul, reserving it for all eternity.

> Having believed you were marked in him
> with a seal, the promised Holy Spirit, who is
> a deposit guaranteeing our inheritance until
> the redemption of those who are God's
> possession—to the praise of his glory. (Eph.
> 1:13, 14)

The promised Holy Spirit marks and seals
the soul, guaranteeing a heavenly inheritance.
No dark power can break the seal that God
places upon a saved soul. The Holy Spirit,
dwelling within, is God's deposit. It is God's
down payment within His possession, which will
be redeemed when the Son of God appears for
us.

God guarantees our place in Heaven, and He
grants us citizenship in Heaven. As citizens of
Heaven, where else would our destiny be but
Heaven?

This is how the apostle Paul put it:

> [O]ur citizenship is in heaven. And we
> eagerly await a Savior from there, the Lord
> Jesus Christ, who, by the power that enables
> him to bring everything under his control,
> will transform our lowly bodies so that they
> will be like his glorious body. (Phil. 3:20, 21)

At the appearing of Christ, He will be seen in
His glorified form, and those who ascend to His
throne shall be like Him. This is our hope of

glory. What gives birth to this phenomenon is the spiritual seed of Christ within.

That spiritual seed also gives birth to an inner transformation in this world: "For God hath not given us the spirit of fear; but of power and of love, and of a sound mind" (2 Tim. 1:7). The Spirit that God gives yields inner power and love. It displaces fear.

This is the catalyst that ignites the inner transformation Paul described: "If the Spirit of him who raised Jesus from the dead is living in you, he who raised Christ from the dead will also give life to your mortal bodies through his Spirit, who lives in you" (Rom. 8:11). When the Spirit that raised Jesus from the dead lives within you, it gives life to your mortal body. This is the renewal, the rebirth caused by the introduction of divine energy (Holy Spirit) from above.

The Holy Spirit within is God's very essence. It is His "divine nature" (2 Peter 1:4). "God has poured out his love into our hearts by the Holy Spirit" (Rom. 5:5), and nothing can "separate us from the love of God that is in Christ Jesus our Lord" (Rom. 8:39). From before the foundation of this world, God planned to give mankind this grace:

> This grace was given us in Christ Jesus before the beginning of time, but it has now been revealed through the appearing of our Savior, Christ Jesus, who has destroyed death and has brought life and immortality to light through the gospel. (2 Tim. 1:9, 10)

Life and immortality are brought to light by Christ's gospel—His words. He brought the message of faith, which Paul declared to us. Paul revealed that Christ enters your life when you invite Him. You invite Him by responding to "the message concerning faith" (Rom. 10:8)—which He gave us:

> [I]f you confess with your mouth, "Jesus is Lord," and believe in your heart that God raised him from the dead, you will be saved. For it is with your heart that you believe and are justified, and it is with your mouth that you confess and are saved. (Rom. 10:9, 10)

When you make the Son of God your own Lord, and believe in the miracle of the Resurrection, your own soul crosses into eternal life. This confession of the heart produces the spiritual birth that overcomes spiritual darkness and yields a place in Christ's spiritual kingdom. To be saved is to be "made sound, to preserve safe from danger [and] loss, and to bring in all positive blessing in the place of condemnation."[7] To be saved is to be born of God. Christ enters your heart by way of the second birth (being born again). It is to be filled with the Holy Spirit. This is exactly what Jesus prophesied while in the Holy Land:

> I [Jesus] will ask the Father and he will give you another Comforter, and he will never

leave you. He is the Holy Spirit, the Spirit who leads into all truth. The world at large cannot receive him, for it isn't looking for him and doesn't recognize him. But you do, for he lives with you now and some day shall be in you. (John 14:16, 17)

When Jesus issued this prophecy, He looked to the day when His followers would be filled with the Holy Spirit, the Comforter. In fact, just days before Christ ascended to the right hand of God, He told His apostles: "For John baptized with water, but in a few days you will be baptized with the Holy Spirit" (Acts 1:5).

The Son of God, as our "great high priest" (Heb. 4:14), sits on the right hand of God, and He baptizes us with the Holy Spirit when the message of faith is believed and confessed. Today, every time someone confesses Jesus as Lord, and believes in the miracle of the Resurrection, that person fulfills Jesus' prophecy.

I fulfilled this prophecy in 1980, in my senior year of college. This is my testimony: There was a girl in my dorm that was not typical. She radiated love, peace, and joy. At first I thought this couldn't be real. I was skeptical. Yet, when I was faced with a crossroads in my life, I came to this conclusion: Only truth could have produced what she radiated. My skepticism ended. My hope began.

I went to her Bible study, and I finally

understood this: Jesus' blood is the sacrifice that I accept to cleanse sin. By making Him Lord of my life, I was exchanging earthly wisdom for divine wisdom. He baptized me with the Holy Spirit and I knew it. I felt a respectful awe for the Creator, and a profound thankfulness for the love, joy, and peace that poured into me through my Lord and His Spirit. His words would now light my path. He was now my Lord. Thank God!

Before you can write your own personal success story, you have to find your voice. If the voice of the Son of God speaks to you and resonates with your voice, then what are you waiting for? Allow yourself to embrace Him as your Lord and Savior.

Confess to Him, "Jesus, I open the door of my heart to you, and ask you to be my Lord and Savior; I accept your sacrifice on the Cross for my sins, and I believe in the miracle of the Resurrection."

With your heart, you believed. Now you are justified (just as if you never sinned).

With your mouth, you confessed. Now you are saved (made whole, reserved for God). This is the message of faith.

Over 35 years ago, I confessed and believed. I realized that there was a new connection with God. God, who is Spirit, created within me another dimension: Holy Spirit, the Comforter. The Spirit created within me fundamentally changed the nature of my being, for that Spirit is eternal, and it is love. It is the very nature of God

Himself: "The fruit of the Spirit is love, joy, peace" (Gal. 5:22). As such, I felt a transformation take place within, as if a fountain of life had sprung open. It was just as Jesus had prophesied: "Whoever drinks the water I give them will never thirst. Indeed, the water I give them will become in them a spring of water welling up to eternal life" (John 4:14). And it was just as Paul had prophesied: "[I]f anyone is in Christ [that is, grafted in, joined to Him by faith in Him as Savior], *he is* a new creature [reborn and renewed by the Holy Spirit]" (2 Cor. 5:17). Now, filled with the Holy Spirit, my Lord empowered me to "pray in the Holy Spirit" (Jude 20), and to speak "by the Spirit of God" (1 Cor. 12:3). (See Chapter 9.)

To speak by the Spirit of God is to have an unmistakable supernatural sign of His indwelling presence.

That changed me.

I knew I had it: eternal life!

It's just as real as our life now. That's what I want you to know without a doubt, because that's what I learned and experienced when God intervened in my life. Until I met the truth, I just didn't know what I didn't know.

When the Messiah baptized me with Holy Spirit I realized that the words on a page of the Bible were no longer just words on a page—they spoke to me. Me.

Jesus Christ said of the Comforter, "He will never leave you." If Christ said the Comforter (Holy Spirit) will never leave me, then how can it leave me? It can't. It's eternal comfort. It's your eternal victory.

This is Christ's gospel of faith, righteousness, and immortality. It is in sharp contrast to the Old Testament, where good works earned righteousness (Deut. 6:25).

This is why the focal point of all human history is Jesus Christ. He declared that mankind had crossed a threshold in the first century. That's why He told Nicodemus about the second spiritual birth. Moses didn't come to bring the spiritual birth—Jesus did.

By way of Jesus, the kingdom of God on Earth finally dawned. Christ declared that He marked the start of the New Covenant from Heaven: "The Law and the Prophets were proclaimed until John [the Baptist]. Since that time, the good news of the kingdom of God is being preached" (Luke 16:16); "For while the Law was given through Moses, grace (unearned, undeserved favor and spiritual blessing) and truth came through Jesus Christ" (John 1:17).

The Son of God brought "the good news of the kingdom of God" which is "grace and truth" (the new agreement). The condemned man who hung on the cross was saved by the Good News, and that Good News is still the Good News.

The Son of God came to Earth to bring this Good News and elevate the standard to that of love and grace: "Jesus [is] the mediator of a new covenant" (Heb. 12:24). Christ fulfilled and voided the Mosaic agreement. Christ "canceled the written code [the Law], with its regulations, that was against us and that stood opposed to us; he took it away, nailing it to the cross" (Col. 2:14). "Christ is the end of the law so that there may be righteousness for everyone who believes" (Rom. 10:4).

Although the Old Testament Law was perfect in its standard, it was opposed to man because it could not change the sin nature that Adam had passed onto him. No one could fulfill it completely because man is imperfect. This is why the people of the Old Testament period sacrificed animals—to cover their sins.

With the Good News of the New Covenant, however, there is no further need to make such sacrifices, because Jesus was the Lamb given by God to cleanse sins, yielding righteousness for everyone who believes. Righteousness comes by faith in the sufficiency of that sacrifice. "For in the gospel, righteousness from God is revealed, a righteousness that is by faith just as it is written: 'The righteous will live by faith'" (Rom. 1:17). This prophecy was fulfilled in Christ. All who open the door to Him receive the "measure of faith" (Rom. 12:3) and "righteousness which is of God by faith" (Phil. 3:9).

On the Cross, Christ took upon Himself all that the world is (sinful), so that souls could become all that He is (righteous): "God made him who had no sin to be sin for us, so that in him we might become the righteousness of God" (2 Cor. 5:21). The righteousness of God is transferred to us through His Son, and there it shall ever remain. Just listen to Jesus' prophecy:

My sheep listen to my voice; I know them, and they follow me. I give them eternal life, and they shall never perish; no one can snatch them out of my hand. My Father, who has given them to me, is greater than all; no one can snatch them out of my Father's hand. (John 10:27–29)

For the Lord gives wisdom;
From His mouth come knowledge and understanding; He stores up sound wisdom for the upright; He is a shield to those who walk uprightly; He guards the paths of justice, And preserves the way of His saints. (Prov. 2:6–8)

2

Treasures: Our Invitation

A new command I give you: Love one another. As I have loved you, so you must love one another. By this all men will know that you are my disciples, if you love one another.

—Jesus Christ (John 13:34, 35)

Beginning with Moses, every prophet recorded something about the coming Messiah, the Christ. And, nearly two thousand years ago, a man named Jesus declared that He was the Son of God. He spoke words that were revolutionary and, frankly, still are revolutionary. Jesus said: "I am the light of the world. He who follows Me shall not walk in darkness, but have the light of life" (John 8:12). Jesus brought to mankind a new agreement from the Creator that addressed the "here and now," and the connection with the "hereafter."

The story of this connection dawned on a most incredible day in human history. The Son of God made His way up a mountainside and sat down. Throngs of followers followed in anticipation. They had no idea that they were about to hear what is now known as the Sermon on the Mount. In His sermon, Jesus handed us our invitation to obtain our true treasure, Heaven's treasures.

Like the first rays of light breaking above a dark horizon, the words of Jesus Christ now form a beacon that reaches across centuries.

The historical record begins:

> Jesus went throughout Galilee, teaching in their synagogues, proclaiming the good news of the kingdom, and healing every disease and sickness among the people. Large crowds from Galilee, the Decapolis, Jerusalem, Judea and the region across the Jordan followed him. Now when Jesus saw the crowds, he went up on a mountainside and sat down. His disciples came to him, and he began to teach them. (Matt. 4:23, 25; 5:1)

Time has no impact on truth. Fast forward two thousand years to the twenty-first century. May we in like manner sit with our eyes fastened on His words. He said:

> Do not store up for yourselves [material] treasures on earth, where moth and rust destroy, and where thieves break in and steal. But store up for yourselves treasures in heaven, where neither moth nor rust destroys, and where thieves do not break in

and steal; for where your treasure is, there your heart [your wishes, your desires; that on which your life centers] will be also. (Matt. 6:19–21)

Why did Jesus issue His invitation during this sermon?

Without question, fundamental truths filled the Sermon on the Mount. Thus, storing up treasures was deemed fundamental by Christ.

After the Son of God handed us His invitation to store up treasures, He directed our steps on how to do so. Jesus told His listeners, "But seek ye first the kingdom of God, and his righteousness; and all these things shall be added unto you" (Matt. 6:33).

Throughout the Sermon on the Mount and the rest of the New Testament, our Lord handed us numerous pictures that express what it means to seek the kingdom of God first and store up treasures. At the heart of storing up treasures is the motivation behind it: unconditional love. Jesus said:

A new command I give you: Love one another. As I have loved you, so you must love one another. By this all men will know that you are my disciples, if you love one another. (John 13:34, 35)

This "love" is divine love (Greek: *Agape*[8]). It is not of this Earth. It has one source, Jesus Christ. We are filled with this love when He baptizes us with the Holy Spirit.

We are vessels, chosen vessels, through which His divine love flows. Once we allow ourselves to embrace this spiritual reality, our truth becomes evident: The love we give is the love of our Lord, and thus we can release the need to seek recognition for it and release the need to gain by it. By embracing a thought pattern such as this, our spiritual walk takes on a new dimension, a new awareness of our personal bond with the Son of God. We are in this together. We have one Lord: Him. We are one with His words.

Giving unconditional love takes many forms, but there are common threads that Christ revealed during His sermon. He said:

> Be careful not to do your acts of righteousness before men, to be seen by them. If you do, you will have no reward from your Father in heaven. So when you give to the needy, do not announce it with trumpets, as the hypocrites do in the synagogues and on the streets, to be honored by men. I tell you the truth, they have received their reward in full. But when you give to the needy, do not let your left hand know what your right hand is doing, so that your giving may be in secret. Then your Father, who sees what is done in secret, will reward you. (Matt. 6:1–4)

In other words, keep your camera crew and

your publicist at home when acting selflessly and giving righteously. God will reward you.

Jesus is communicating not only a difference in the source of the reward, but the source of the inspiration: "for where your treasure is, there your heart [your wishes, your desires; that on which your life centers] will be also." The "heart" (literally, "the seat of life"9) is the starting point of our decisions and personal developments that produce our unique, distinctive character. The heart is the inner voice that directs our steps and speaks volumes about what we value. It is the center of our longing, devotion, and desire.

What we choose to store in our heart becomes evident, now and for eternity. Thus, "Keep thy heart with all diligence; for out of it are the issues of life" (Prov. 4:23). To "keep" means, "to guard, protect, and maintain."10

We create an internal atmosphere and inner dialogue in our heart by guarding, protecting, and maintaining eternal, divine truths. This internal creation in our heart, or inner dialogue, eventually creates what is outside of us. If our heart becomes an unfailing spiritual compass, with our true north pointing upward to Heaven, then we are seeking God's glory.

Storing up treasures in Heaven is a journey through which we "see" God and His glory in the divine light in which Jesus presented Him. Jesus said, "He who has seen Me has seen the Father" (John 14:9). When Jesus speaks, He presents the heart of our Creator.

Jesus was God's gift to us. Jesus loved the unlovable. He ate with sinners and gave up His life for us. We know intuitively that His love is the most endearing love. It is love without conditions. We see this in the example He gave us:

> And if anyone gives even a cup of cold water to one of these little ones because he is my disciple, I tell you the truth, he will certainly not lose his reward. (Matt. 10:42)

That's storing up treasures. These are acts of righteousness and compassion. Simple? Yes!

But it's not just simple, it's fundamental. It's fundamental to the Sermon on the Mount and fundamental to the doctrine of the New Covenant.

In Jesus' sermon, He focused on walking in His light, drawing a contrast between finite human love (which seeks a reward on Earth) and infinite divine love (which does not seek a reward on Earth). In essence, it is the difference between human vanity and human valor.

The Son of God set the stage and gave us our storyline: Be free of the world's ways. Be free of thoughts that separate us from the mind of Christ. Be wholly dedicated to elevating our will to His will. In this light, Christ said:

> And when you pray, do not be like the hypocrites, for they love to pray standing in the synagogues and on the street corners to

be seen by men. I tell you the truth, they have received their reward in full. But when you pray, go into your room, close the door and pray to your Father, who is unseen. Then your Father, who sees what is done in secret, will reward you. (Matt. 6:5, 6)

Our Lord is asking us: Why seek a reward in the sight of men? Forget that temptation. Prayer and works that are done solely to gain points on Earth will score a zero on God's scale. "When you pray, go into your room, close the door and pray to your Father, who is unseen. Then your Father, who sees what is done in secret, will reward you."

Consider the Psalms, and what is said about opening our hearts: "My sacrifice, O God, is a broken spirit" (Ps. 51:17). A "broken" (or "burst"[11]) spirit is one that is broken open and cries out to God, a loving Father. In that cry is a way of being.

This way of being is our "sacrifice"; it is our righteous way (forward). Consider the Psalms, and the inner dialogue of a troubled soul: "Why, my soul, are you downcast? Why so disturbed within me? Put your hope in God, for I will yet praise him, my Savior and my God" (Ps. 43:5). The Psalmist is telling his soul to "wake up"; he is telling his soul to put its hope in God. That is our righteous way (forward).

Being honest and open with God draws you closer to Him because you leave your pride and self-reliance at the door when you enter into your room to pray.

King David was a man after God's own heart (Acts 13:22), and David found solace in revealing his inner dialogue to God when his soul was troubled.

Exactly how do we open up to God? Christ's revelation about approaching the throne of God is our guide:

> Therefore, since we have a great high priest who has ascended into heaven, Jesus the Son of God, let us hold firmly to the faith we profess. For we do not have a high priest who is unable to empathize with our weaknesses, but we have one who has been tempted in every way, just as we are—yet he did not sin. Let us then approach God's throne of grace with confidence, so that we may receive mercy and find grace to help us in our time of need. (Heb. 4:14–16)

Jesus Christ is our great high priest who understands our human frailty. In that frailty, we recognize our weakness and God's strength. In prayer, there is an expectation that God will bear His mighty arm—and bring His power, love, mercy, and grace into our lives. There is also an expectation to embrace His will.

Consider an answer to prayer given to Paul by Christ. Christ said: "My grace is sufficient for you [My lovingkindness and My mercy are more than enough—always available—regardless of the situation]; for [My] power is being perfected [and is completed and shows itself most effectively] in [your] weakness" (2 Cor. 12:9).

We pray before His throne with confidence, seeking grace and mercy. We just need to expect it in way that is most beneficial: from His heavenly perspective.

Storing up treasures in Heaven is bringing a heavenly perspective to all we think, do, pray, and say. Jesus said: "Love your neighbor as yourself" (Luke 10:27).

After Jesus gave this command to love, He received a question: "And who is my neighbor?" (Luke 10:30). Jesus responded with a parable:

"A man was going down from Jerusalem to Jericho, when he was attacked by robbers. They stripped him of his clothes, beat him and went away, leaving him half dead. A priest happened to be going down the same road, and when he saw the man, he passed by on the other side. So too, a Levite, when he came to the place and saw him, passed by on the other side. But a Samaritan, as he traveled, came where the man was; and when he saw him, he took pity on him. He went to him and bandaged his wounds, pouring on oil and wine. Then he put the man on his own donkey, brought him to an inn and took care of him. The next day he took out two denarii and gave them to the innkeeper. 'Look after him,' he said, 'and when I return, I will reimburse you for any extra expense you may have.' Which of these three do you think was a neighbor to the man who fell into the hands of robbers?" The expert in the law replied, "The one who had mercy on him." Jesus told him, "Go and do likewise." (Luke 10:30–37)

"Go and do likewise." The Good Samaritan walked down the road and saw a divine response. In a similar manner, if we step into life and see treasures in Heaven, then we have embraced a divine response to what we see.

Listen to what Paul said regarding a divine response:

Command those who are rich in this present world not to be arrogant nor to put their hope in wealth, which is so uncertain, but to put their hope in God, who richly provides us with everything for our enjoyment. Command them to do good, to be rich in good deeds, and to be generous and willing to share. In this way they will lay up treasure for themselves as a firm foundation for the coming age, so that they may take hold of the life that is truly life. (1 Tim. 6:17–19)

To put our hope in our God is to know our true wealth. It is to trust our Creator and not the wealth we create.

Paul said: "to do good," and "to be rich in good deeds," and "to be generous and willing to share." And he said: "In this way they will lay up treasure for themselves as a firm foundation for the coming age, so that they may take hold of the life that is truly life."

"[T]he coming age," which literally means, "impending future,"[12] refers to the time when prophecies about the future are fulfilled. Ultimately, it is a time when our King—who currently reigns in Heaven—will reign on the new Earth and we will reign with Him. Our Creator will bring forth a new reality, which is the grand finale for His eternal kingdom: paradise, the new Earth. Storing up treasures builds a firm foundation for this coming age.

What is a "firm foundation"? It is a foundation you want.

What is life that is "truly life"? You could ask this question a hundred times and it would yield a hundred different answers. Yet, according to Christ the King, life that is truly life is found by perceiving mortal existence in light of eternal realities.

With these two concepts, "a firm foundation" and a "life that is truly life," Paul revealed the connection between the "here and now" and the "hereafter." If we build on the foundation of Christ in this life, then we build a firm foundation for the next life.

To build on the foundation of Christ is to build into your life a way of being: the way of unconditional love.

Jesus said:

Love the Lord your God with all your heart

and with all your soul and with all your mind and with all your strength. (Mark 12:30)

Love your neighbor as yourself. (Luke 10:27)

Love one another. As I have loved you, so you must love one another. (John 13:34)

And Jesus said this:

Ask, and it will be given to you; seek, and you will find; knock, and it will be opened to you. For everyone who asks receives, and he who seeks finds, and to him who knocks it will be opened. (Matt. 7:7, 8)

And then Jesus compared imperfect mankind to our Heavenly Father:

If you then, evil (sinful by nature) as you are, know how to give good and advantageous gifts to your children, how much more will your Father who is in heaven [perfect as He is] give what is good and advantageous to those who keep on asking Him. (Matt. 7:11)

Whoever is kind to the poor lends to the Lord, and he will reward them for what they have done. (Prov. 19:17)

3

Treasures: Eternal Crowns

I [Paul] have fought the good fight, I have finished the race, I have kept the faith. Now there is in store for me the crown of righteousness, which the Lord, the righteous Judge, will award to me on that day—and not only to me, but also to all who have longed for his appearing.

—The Apostle Paul (2 Tim. 4:7, 8)

Throughout the New Testament, our King presented different pieces of the treasure puzzle to different apostles. The writings of Peter, James, John, and Paul, reveal a picture of Heaven's riches, the eternal crowns. Christ the King shall "crown" righteous souls in His kingdom with "life," "righteousness," "glory," and "rejoicing." Each of these "qualities" represents "crowns" of everlasting heavenly honor, and our King shall bestow these crowns, based on what is accomplished through His holy name on Earth.

By way of His invitation to store up treasures, the Son of God heralded the connection between the "here and now" and the "hereafter." Divine revelation reveals eternal remembrance by a loving God, taking the form of eternal crowns—all earned by giving unconditional love in different ways. In essence, Christ's revelation about treasures provides inspiration and direction for the love we give.

The Crown of Life

James wrote:

Blessed is the man who perseveres under trial, because when he has stood the test, he will receive the crown of life that God has promised to those who love him. When tempted, no one should say, "God is tempting me." For God cannot be tempted by evil, nor does he tempt anyone; but each one is tempted when, by his own evil desire, he is dragged away and enticed. Every good and perfect gift is from above, coming down from the Father of the heavenly lights, who does not change like shifting shadows. (James 1:12–14, 17)

The word "trial" means "putting to the test."[13] If we live the truth, we will encounter tribulation. Our Lord knows this and knows us. He knows that the truth about treasures in Heaven will leave an impression upon our hearts. Thus, it makes perfect sense that He would hand us unique inspiration to overcome unique challenges. In that inspiration, deliverance is found.

In the midst of a trial, "no one should say, 'God is tempting me.'" Our faithfulness to our God includes rejecting the notion that He would tempt His own children. In the Garden of Eden, Satan, not God, did the tempting. "God is light; in him there is no darkness at all" (1 John 1:5). The Almighty is absolute light; therefore, temptation is darkness. With this knowledge, we are empowered to think clearly in the midst of a trial.

Persevering through a trial is an example of unconditionally loving our King—but also unconditionally loving ourselves. Why? You defy the circumstances. You don't let the circumstances determine how you really feel about yourself. You love yourself no matter what the conditions. Because of His love, you love yourself unconditionally. This is a way of being found deep within the heart. It can remain unshaken by drawing upon the truth of who we are in the kingdom, and drawing upon the specific revelation to persevere in a trial.

This divine revelation can only bring forth comfort. This is how knowledge affects our will. It is a blessing to know that God isn't the cause of our temptation. Our Creator is the giver of "good and perfect gifts." He is not the source of tribulation upon the righteous. He is the source of comfort and deliverance.

Blessed be the God and Father of our Lord

Jesus Christ, the Father of sympathy (pity and mercy) and the God [Who is the Source] of every comfort (consolation and encouragement), Who comforts (consoles and encourages) us in every trouble (calamity and affliction), so that we may also be able to comfort (console and encourage) those who are in any kind of trouble or distress, with the comfort (consolation and encouragement) with which we ourselves are comforted (consoled and encouraged) by God. For just as Christ's [own] sufferings fall to our lot [as they overflow upon His disciples, and we share and experience them] abundantly, so through Christ comfort (consolation and encouragement) is also [shared and experienced] abundantly by us. (2 Cor. 1:3–5)

This is how Peter put it:

In all this [work of God] you greatly rejoice, though now for a little while you may have had to suffer grief in all kinds of trials. These have come so that the proven genuineness of your faith—of greater worth than gold, which perishes even though refined by fire— may result in praise, glory and honor when Jesus Christ is revealed. (1 Peter 1:6, 7)

Trials bring forth "the proven genuineness of your faith" resulting in "praise, glory and honor." Trials prove us. They test our mettle.

We beat the trial—it doesn't beat us. Let that be our testimony.

Regarding perseverance, Christ Himself said: "be thou faithful unto death, and I will give thee a crown of life" (Rev. 2:10).

Compare this to what James said: "When he has stood the test, he will receive the crown of life that God has promised to those who love him" (James 1:12). The parallel between Jesus and James is unmistakable. In this life, to "stand the test" is to be "faithful unto death"—and that is what it means to "love him."

Why else would our Lord give us this revelation if not to inspire us?!

Let me say this about a trial: Just prior to the divine intervention in the year 2000, I faced a headwind on my path that knocked me off my feet. My life became a trial. It tested every ounce of my strength. I had to lean heavily on everyone around me, especially my family. I had to lean on the truth—and lean on the source of that truth: God.

I knew in my heart of hearts that perseverance was my only true option. Then, out of nowhere, God intervened. From February 24, 2000 to April 6, 2000, He reached down and got my attention. He transformed me. He showed me one supernatural event after another. His intervention guided me straight into the Scriptures.

By April 6, I no longer faced a headwind. He filled my sails with a heavenly breeze. Where I was once dead in the water, He created a new sailing lane, a new path. I moved to a cottage by a lake and began writing.

My prayer had been answered. My Lord made a way where there was no way. He opened doors I thought were locked. My Lord handed me the time, inspiration, and direction to dive into the Scriptures, in particular, Revelation.

My trial was over. My new chapter in life began.

Look at what Paul said about how our God works with us during trying times:

> No temptation [regardless of its source] has overtaken or enticed you that is not common to human experience [nor is any temptation unusual or beyond human resistance]; but God is faithful [to His word—He is compassionate and trustworthy], and He will not let you be tempted beyond your ability [to resist], but along with the temptation He [has in the past and is now and] will [always] provide the way out as well, so that you will be able to endure it [without yielding, and will overcome temptation with joy]. (1 Cor. 10:13)

God made a way for me to escape to a safe landing place. His Words about perseverance were not just words. They spoke to me. Me.

His words provide something so needed when we are facing life head on: We never suffer for naught. Trust God and take "the proven genuineness of your faith" to the throne of Christ.

Without question, Jesus was put to the test just by telling the truth in the face of those who didn't want it. In the Sermon on the Mount, Jesus declared fundamental truths about unconditional love and divine remembrance, including the connection between trials and rewards.

> Blessed are those who are persecuted because of righteousness, for theirs is the kingdom of heaven. Blessed are you when people insult you, persecute you and falsely say all kinds of evil against you because of me. Rejoice and be glad, because great is your reward in heaven, for in the same way they persecuted the prophets who were before you. (Matt. 5:10–12)

> With His divine insight, we are armed.
> With His example, we are inspired.

> [L]ooking unto Jesus, the author and finisher of our faith, who for the joy that was set before Him endured the cross, despising the shame, and has sat down at the right hand of the throne of God. (Heb. 12:2)

> Jesus saw the joy. He persevered.
> If you are in the midst of a trial, keep going.

> [D]o not throw away your confidence; it will

be richly rewarded. You need to persevere so that when you have done the will of God, you will receive what he has promised. (Heb. 10:35, 36)

The Crown of Glory

Following His Resurrection, Jesus met with His apostles and spoke of caring for His flock. To Peter, Jesus asked, "'Simon [Peter] son of John, do you truly love me?' He answered, 'Yes, Lord, you know that I love you.' Jesus said, 'Take care of my sheep'" (John 21:16).

Years after this conversation with Jesus, Peter wrote about it, declaring that the crown of glory awaits those who impart the truth as good shepherds.

To the elders among you, I appeal as a fellow elder, a witness of Christ's sufferings and one who also will share in the glory to be revealed: Be shepherds of God's flock that is under your care, serving as overseers—not because you must, but because you are willing, as God wants you to be; not greedy for money, but eager to serve; not lording it over those entrusted to you, but being examples to the flock. And when the Chief Shepherd appears, you will receive the crown of glory that will never fade away. (1 Peter 5:1–4)

As with Peter, each one in the kingdom holds a unique place in God's mind. Likewise, each one can have a unique impact on the hearts and minds of those within one's sphere of influence. It is the calling of God to respond with the unconditional love that God places in the heart, nurturing and comforting with the truth.

With regard to caring for the flock of Christ, the unconditional love we give affects what we speak, and what we don't speak. Paul spoke of not judging one another by not comparing one another.

In a letter to the church, He had to write about those in the church who were doing just that: judging. Paul said:

[W]hen they [in the church] measure themselves with themselves and compare themselves with one another, they are without understanding and behave unwisely. (2 Cor. 10:12)

To compare one with another is to judge; it is to behave unwisely. In the kingdom of Christ, we are all equipped to bring our own unique DNA, love, strength, knowledge, and wisdom to the table of our King. Caring for the flock includes not comparing one with another in the kingdom.

As members of Christ's church, we are also members of the body of Christ. As such, each part has its own role to play. Paul said: "Just as a body, though one, has many parts, but all its many parts form one body, so it is with Christ. Now you are the body of Christ, and each one of you is a part of it" (1 Cor. 12:12, 27).

Everyone in the kingdom is a unique part in the body of Christ, with their own vital function. Don't give into the temptation to judge according to appearances.

Along with the temptation to judge is the temptation not to forgive. Jesus spoke of forgiveness in unforgettable terms.

> Peter came to Him and said, "Lord, how often shall my brother sin against me, and I forgive him? Up to seven times?" Jesus said to him, "I do not say to you, up to seven times, but up to seventy times seven." (Matt. 18:21, 22)

In essence, Jesus said to Peter: let forgiveness be a part of your way of being.

Consider a story in the Gospels: the woman caught in adultery. With this story, we are handed a contrast: the "eyes" of Christ and the "eyes" of the accusers. Her accusers wanted to judge and stone her. In contrast, Jesus said "Let him who is without sin among you be the first to throw a stone at her" (John 8:7). No stones were thrown, and the woman was set free with this thought: "sin no more" (John 8:11).

Christ loved unconditionally with spiritual eyes.

Human interaction is fraught with imperfection. Who hasn't been on the receiving end of being wronged?

This is the message we brand in our minds: If the blood of Jesus brought complete forgiveness of sin, then we can't forget where we came from. Jesus forgave our past sins. Now we forgive forward. As we all know, forgiveness frees the one who offers forgiveness.

Only truth can make one free, and the Lord will recognize those who gave the truth and lived it.

The Crown of Righteousness

Paul revealed this: If we live our lives such that we long for the appearance of our Lord, a crown of righteousness awaits.

> I [Paul] have fought the good fight, I have finished the race, I have kept the faith. Now there is in store for me the crown of righteousness, which the Lord, the righteous Judge, will award to me on that day—and not only to me, but also to all who have longed for his appearing. (2 Tim. 4:7, 8)

If we have "fought the good fight," "finished the race," and "kept the faith," then we will long for "His appearing" as well. If we long for that day, then we will long to stand before the throne of Christ.

Paul blazed a trail for those in the kingdom to follow. He ran the race of life with a single-minded goal: victory. To describe his life, he offered an athletic analogy: "I have fought the good fight." Paul was a "spiritual athlete" who fought with "the sword of the Spirit, which is the word of God" (Eph. 6:17). He lived for the sake of the Gospel, the Good News.

> I do this for the sake of the good news (the Gospel), in order that I may become a participator in it and share in its [blessings along with you]. Do you not know that in a race all the runners compete, but [only] one receives the prize? So run [your race] that you may lay hold [of the prize] and make it yours. Now every athlete who goes into training conducts himself temperately and restricts himself in all things. They do it to win a wreath that will soon wither, but we [do it to receive a crown of eternal blessedness] that cannot wither. (1 Cor. 9:23–25)

Paul conducted himself "temperately," which means to exercise mastery. By doing so, he maximized the meaning of his life. He kept the faith by not diluting the Gospel that produced that faith. His conscience was captive to the truth.

Paul didn't compete for money, or status, or an earthly crown, but for "a crown of eternal blessedness." Eternal blessedness applies to all four crowns, because that is what they all bring: eternal blessedness.

Paul lived his life in the name of truth. As an athlete, he sliced through the spiritual darkness that pervaded the world in the first century. He held to the will of God and derived strength from his fixed mindset. He had the absolute assurance that his Lord would remember him and all in the kingdom who lived for the unseen, greater good.

All in the kingdom are citizens of Heaven; it makes perfect sense that we would store up treasures in Heaven. Paul said:

> Since, then, you have been raised with Christ, set your hearts on things above, where Christ is seated at the right hand of God. Set your minds [your affection] on things above, not on earthly things. (Col. 3:1, 2)

To store up treasures is to seek those things which are above, and we do so by seeing with spiritual eyes on Earth.

Let Paul's declaration be our declaration: "[I]f only I may finish the race and complete the task the Lord Jesus has given me—the task of testifying to the gospel of God's grace" (Acts 20:24).

When the Lord Jesus Christ returns, He shall crown His flock not only with life, glory, and righteousness, but also with rejoicing.

The Crown of Rejoicing

The fourth crown is connected to Jesus' prophecy: "Blessed are those who hunger and thirst for righteousness, for they will be filled" (Matt. 5:6). This prophecy is fulfilled in those who embrace the Good News of the gospel of God's grace.

Paul's prophecy about this crown pertains to those who are filled with His righteousness:

> [W]hat is our hope, or joy, or crown of rejoicing? Are not even ye in the presence of our Lord Jesus Christ at his coming? For ye are our glory and joy. (1 Thess. 2:19, 20)

Paul rejoiced with those who believed the Good News. They are his glory. They are his joy. They will be his crown of rejoicing. Paul established this truth when he said: "my brothers, you whom I love and long for, my joy and crown" (Phil. 4:1).

Pure joy poured forth from Paul's soul, knowing that the Good News he shared produced eternal results: souls entering the kingdom of Christ.

Of this salvation of souls, Jesus said, "I tell you, there is rejoicing in the presence of the angels of God over one sinner who repents" (Luke 15:10). James said, "let him know that he who turns a sinner from the error of his way will save a soul from death and cover a multitude of sins" (James 5:20).

In my 35 years of reaching out to souls, talking about divine truth has produced immense and lasting fulfillment. I have found it rewarding beyond measure.

I recall two individuals who had lost their interest in life. Each desired to leave this world. However, when each believed the message of faith, each gained a solid foundation, the rock, Christ Jesus. God put me in the right place at the right time to reach them, the same way the woman from college was perfectly placed to reach me. Talk about a life that is truly life.

God enabled me to speak His Good News and see lives change right before my eyes because the truth set them "free" (John 8:32), just as it had me. That is what Jesus came to bring: Good News. Look at how He described His mission:

> The Spirit of the Lord is upon me, because he hath anointed me to preach the gospel to the poor; he hath sent me to heal the brokenhearted, to preach deliverance to the captives, and recovering of sight to the blind, to set at liberty them that are bruised. (Luke 4:18)

His message reached me. Now I speak it.

Paul painted this picture of speaking the truth by referring to himself as a servant in the field of God. Paul, along with a fellow co-worker,

Apollos, planted and watered seeds of truth.

> What, after all, is Apollos? And what is Paul? Only servants, through whom you came to believe—as the Lord has assigned to each his task. I planted the seed, Apollos watered it, but God made it grow. So neither he who plants nor he who waters is anything, but only God, who makes things grow. The man who plants and the man who waters have one purpose, and each will be rewarded according to his own labor. For we are God's fellow workers; you are God's field, God's building. (1 Cor. 3:5–9)

God will remember who planted and watered His field: the Earth. We plant the message of faith, which yields "the righteousness that comes from God and is by faith" (Phil. 3:9).

Paul had his moment in time during the first century A.D. Consider what Christ told him: "I am sending you to them to open their eyes and turn them from darkness to light, and from the power of Satan to God, so that they may receive forgiveness of sins and a place among those who are sanctified by faith in me" (Acts 26:17, 18).

Today, we are the "ambassadors for Christ" (2 Cor. 5:20). Thus, "Always be prepared to give an answer to everyone who asks you to give the reason for the hope that you have. But do this with gentleness and respect" (1 Peter 3:15).

The legacy of Christ and His apostles is ours to carry forth. Let our generation be remembered for being worthy of such a high calling.

We only have one soul, one life, with which to live in this world of finite time. Clearly, anything that is counterproductive to God cannot yield Heaven's blessing in the future world. Our Lord implores us: Live life as if it matters for all eternity—because it does.

Our King: His Exhortation

The final word given in the New Testament about our crowns is given by our King Himself: "I am coming soon. Hold on to what you have, so that no one will take your crown" (Rev. 3:11). Beloved, let no one talk you out of seeking treasures in Heaven or talk you into minimizing the importance of it. If the future appearing of our King shall unveil all that currently waits in Heaven, then the only reasonable response is to live for it.

> Look to yourselves (take care) that you may not lose (throw away or destroy) all that we and you have labored for, but that you may [persevere until you] win and receive back a perfect reward [in full]. (2 John 8)

A good name is more desirable than great riches; to be esteemed is better than silver or gold. (Prov. 22:1)

ACT TWO

4

The Appearance of Our King

> The sun will be turned to darkness and the moon to blood before the coming of the great and glorious day of the Lord. And everyone who calls on the name of the Lord will be saved.
>
> —The Apostle Peter (Acts 2:20, 21)

J ust as our Lord revealed different pieces of the treasure puzzle to Peter, John, and Paul, He did likewise with each apostle regarding His future appearing for His kingdom. Each piece of the puzzle comes together forming a unified picture of this coming glorious day—which is called, "the day of the Lord Jesus Christ" (1 Cor.1:8). When Christ does appear in the sky, it will signal the harvest of His kingdom from Earth to Heaven.

The Apostle Peter

On a most significant day in human

history—almost two thousand years ago—Jesus Christ poured out the Holy Spirit upon the Earth, and on that day, Peter spoke forth a prophecy about the future appearing of Christ the King. Peter quoted the Old Testament prophet Joel:

> The sun will be turned to darkness and the moon to blood before the coming of the great and glorious day of the Lord. And everyone who calls on the name of the Lord will be saved. (Acts 2:20, 21)

On this day—the first day of the church—Peter prophesied about the future salvation of the church. On the "day of the Lord," "everyone who calls on the name of the Lord will be saved." That's us: the King's kingdom. We are the ones born of God, filled with the Holy Spirit, who entered the eternal kingdom which calls on the name of the Lord. Every prophecy about the future salvation of Christ's kingdom (the church) is founded upon, and is in complete agreement with, Peter's prophecy.

The Apostle Paul

To the apostle Paul, Christ revealed exactly what shall transpire on the day of the Lord Jesus Christ. Whereas Peter foresaw celestial signs, Paul foresaw the impact upon the kingdom of Christ when it is actually harvested from the

Earth. To Paul, Christ revealed the glory that shall accompany His return in the sky. Those who died in Christ will be resurrected, and those who are alive will be transformed immortal.

> The Lord himself will come down from heaven, with a loud command, with the voice of the archangel and with the trumpet call of God, and the dead in Christ will rise first. After that, we who are still alive and are left will be caught up together with them in the clouds to meet the Lord in the air. And so we will be with the Lord forever. (1 Thess. 4:16, 17)

With the voice of the archangel, Christ shall issue a "loud command": It's time! Sleeping souls will rise from the grave made to be imperishable, and living souls shall be transformed, made to be immortal. All of them will be "caught up," or raptured. (Rapture is derived from the Latin verb *Rapiermur*[14] found in the Latin translation of the Bible, known as the Vulgate.)

All raptured souls will ascend to the clouds in a supernatural form that matches the molecular structure of Christ Himself. It is a structure unlike anything on Earth, for it is of heavenly content. This is how Paul put it:

> There are also heavenly bodies and there are earthly bodies; but the splendor of the heavenly bodies is one kind, and the

splendor of the earthly bodies is another.
The sun has one kind of splendor, the moon
another and the stars another; and star
differs from star in splendor. So will it be
with the resurrection of the dead. The body
that is sown is perishable, it is raised
imperishable; it is sown in dishonor, it is
raised in glory; it is sown in weakness, it is
raised in power; it is sown a natural body, it
is raised a spiritual body. If there is a natural
body, there is also a spiritual body. And just
as we have borne the likeness of the earthly
man, so shall we bear the likeness of the
man from heaven. (1 Cor. 15:40–44, 49)

Listen very carefully, I tell you a mystery [a
secret truth decreed by God and previously
hidden, but now revealed]; we will not all
sleep [in death], but we will all be
[completely]   changed   [wondrously
transformed], in a moment, in the twinkling
of an eye, at [the sound of] the last trumpet
call. For a trumpet will sound, and the dead
[who believed in Christ] will be raised
imperishable, and we will be [completely]
changed [wondrously transformed].For this
perishable [part of us] must put on the
imperishable [nature], and this mortal [part
of us that is capable of dying] must put on
immortality [which is freedom from death].
(1 Cor. 15:51–53)

The power of Christ shall break the bonds of

mortality and free souls for eternity. By revelation Christ said that He would take a natural body of flesh and blood and transform it into a powerful, eternal, and spiritual body, thereby defeating death forever. Paul prophesied:

> When the perishable has been clothed with the imperishable, and the mortal with immortality, then the saying that is written will come true: "Death has been swallowed up in victory." (1 Cor. 15:54)
> O death, where is thy sting? O grave, where is thy victory? (1 Cor. 15:55)

In his prophecy, Paul quoted two Old Testament prophets: Isaiah and Hosea. Isaiah prophesied: "He will swallow up death in victory" (Isa. 25:8). Hosea prophesied: "Where are your plagues, death; where is your destruction, Sh'ol [the grave]?" (Hosea 13:14).

Paul finished this prophecy of Christ's victory over death with this exhortation:

> [T]hanks be to God, who gives us the victory through our Lord Jesus Christ. Therefore, my beloved brethren, be steadfast, immovable, always abounding in the work of the Lord, knowing that your labor is not in vain in the Lord. (1 Cor. 15:58)

We are to see the appearance of our Lord as clearly as we see the present moment. This clarity produces a transforming vision for our own lives now. Our righteous works are not in vain. We revel in the future because God is already there.

We are to see this world not continuing as man would have it, but as God will have it after He intervenes. This is apocalyptic thinking. It refers to the intervention of God's Son into human affairs. In our case, it is the Rapture.

Paul added to our understanding of the Rapture by revealing another piece of the puzzle: The day of the Lord will come upon the world suddenly. Paul prophesied:

> Now, brothers and sisters, about times and dates we do not need to write to you, for you know very well that the day of the Lord will come like a thief in the night. [Y]ou, brothers and sisters, are not in darkness so that this day should surprise you like a thief. You are all children of the light and children of the day. God did not appoint us to suffer wrath but to receive salvation through our Lord Jesus Christ. (1 Thess. 5:1, 2, 4, 5, 9)

Arriving like "a thief in the night," the day of the Lord will come upon the world with a sudden surprise. Paul prophesied about "times and dates," not the lack of signs.

Those in the kingdom—"the children of the light and children of the day"—will be raptured suddenly, but it will not come as a surprise. The kingdom is expecting their King.

In this same prophecy, Paul revealed another critical component of the Rapture: The kingdom will be harvested from this Earth *before* God judges the world during the time known as "the wrath." Without question, Paul began his prophecy with the Rapture (1 Thess. 4:16, 17), and ended his prophecy by declaring Christ's kingdom is saved from the wrath (1 Thess. 5:9). His prophecy presents a unified picture: The "effect" of being saved from the wrath has an unmistakable "cause," the Rapture. Just as God alerted and rescued Noah prior to the flood, Christ has alerted and shall rescue His kingdom prior to the wrath.

Christ's kingdom is rescued from the coming judgment (or wrath), because as Paul said, "being justified by his blood, we shall be saved from wrath through him" (Rom. 5:9). By way of the cleansing blood of Jesus, the kingdom is already judged righteous in Christ. This is why the kingdom is saved from the judgment that is coming upon the world. Thus, the Rapture is a pre-wrath Rapture.

The timing of the Rapture, in relation to end-time events, is confirmed by the revelation Christ gave to John.

The Apostle John

There is only one other place in the New Testament where the sun turns black and the moon turns blood red: Revelation (also known as the Book of Revelation). When the sixth seal of Revelation opens, the signs in the sun and moon will usher in the day of the Lord—and the Rapture of the kingdom.

> I [John] watched as he opened the sixth seal. There was a great earthquake. The sun turned black like sackcloth made of goat hair, the whole moon turned blood red, and the stars in the sky fell to earth, as figs drop from a fig tree when shaken by a strong wind. The heavens receded like a scroll being rolled up, and every mountain and island was removed from its place. (Rev. 6:12–14)

When darkness surrounds the planet, the moon turns blood red, stars shoot upon the horizon, and every mountain and island shift from a massive earthquake, the deceptive calm upon Earth shall end abruptly. All the world will see "the face of him who sits on the throne" (Rev. 6:16). With this colossal presentation, Heaven shall put the nations on notice that a threshold has been reached: Divine intervention will harvest the kingdom from the Earth.

In a vision, John saw a picture of this future glory, when the kingdom shall stand before their Lord.

> After this I looked, and there before me was a great multitude that no one could count, from every nation, tribe, people and

language, standing before the throne and before the Lamb. They were wearing white robes and were holding palm branches in their hands. And they cried out in a loud voice: "Salvation belongs to our God, who sits on the throne, and to the Lamb."

All the angels were standing around the throne and around the elders and the four living creatures. They fell down on their faces before the throne and worshiped God, saying "Amen! Praise and glory and wisdom and thanks and honor and power and strength be to our God forever and ever. Amen!"

Then one of the elders asked me, "These in white robes—who are they, and where did they come from?"

I answered, "Sir, you know." And he said, "These are they who have come out of the great tribulation; they have washed their robes and made them white in the blood of the Lamb. Therefore, they are before the throne of God and serve him day and night in his temple; and he who sits on the throne will shelter them with his presence. 'Never again will they hunger; never again will they thirst. The sun will not beat down on them,' nor any scorching heat. For the Lamb at the center of the throne will be their shepherd; 'he will lead them to springs of living water.'

'And God will wipe away every tear from their eyes.'" (Rev. 7:9–17)

This harvest of souls—gathered before the Lamb of God—will shout the victory cry: "Salvation belongs to our God, who sits on the throne, and to the Lamb." That's us! This is what Peter meant when he said we shall be saved on the day of the Lord. All who call on the name of the Lord will be saved when He appears in the sky. The heavens—filled with His kingdom—will recede like a scroll being rolled up.

Like Peter, John prophesied that the sun will turn black and the moon will turn blood red (Rev. 6:12). Like Paul, John prophesied of Christ's appearance in the clouds: "Behold, He is coming with the clouds, and every eye will see Him" (Rev. 1:7). Every eye on Earth will know that this is His day to intervene in human affairs—and change the course of human history. All this will come to pass when the sixth seal opens—which is before the time of judgment (wrath) which begins with the seventh seal. (See the Epilogue.)

John unveiled revelation never before revealed, but like Peter and Paul, John also quoted the Old Testament (Isaiah). Isaiah prophesied:

They will neither hunger nor thirst, nor will the desert heat or the sun beat down on them. He who has compassion on them will guide them and lead them beside springs of water. (Isa. 49:10)

The Sovereign Lord will wipe away the tears from all faces. (Isa. 25:8)

The Rapture: A Mystery

John quoted Isaiah. Peter quoted Joel. Paul quoted Hosea and Isaiah.

It wasn't until the days of the first century A.D. that Peter, Paul, and John quoted and revealed the mystery of the Rapture hidden in the Old Testament. Peter, Paul, and John all quoted Old Testament prophets; and, by doing so, they unfolded prophecies that God had hidden in the Old Testament. They were hidden because God hid the prophetic meaning from the Old Testament prophets. God had to keep the Rapture a mystery (hidden from His enemies) so His plan for His kingdom would unfold to perfection. That's why Paul referred to the Rapture as a "mystery" (1 Cor. 15:51).

The apostles added unique pieces of the prophetic puzzle, combining Old Testament prophecy and New Testament revelation. Together, the apostles presented the complete picture of the coming Rapture.

Look at John's prophecy of this coming day:

Beloved, we are [even here and] now God's children; it is not yet disclosed (made clear) what we shall be [hereafter], but we know that when He comes and is manifested, we shall [as God's children] resemble *and* be like Him, for we shall see Him just as He [really] is. (1 John 3:2)

In the way of righteousness there is life; along that path is immortality. (Prov. 12:28)

5

Treasures: The *Bema*

And all the assemblies (churches) shall recognize and understand that I am He Who searches minds (the thoughts, feelings, and purposes) and the [inmost] hearts, and I will give to each of you [the reward for what you have done] as your work deserves.

—Jesus Christ (Rev. 2:23)

F rom the throne of the King, the Judgment Seat, Christ will judge His kingdom, determining the impartation of His reward. Christ's Judgment Seat is often referred to by its Greek name the *Bema,* which means, "a raised place, a tribune to speak from in a public assembly."[15] It is the victory stage from which judgment is cast and rewards are bestowed.

In the case of the *Bema*, the members of the King's kingdom are the assembly. It is at the *Bema*, the victory stage, that Christ will bestow Heaven's treasures. To present the glory of what shall come to pass at the *Bema*, Christ unveiled visions to Paul and John.

John described this coming scene of future

glory this way:

> After this I looked, and there before me was
> a great multitude that no one could count,
> from every nation, tribe, people and
> language, standing before the throne and
> before the Lamb. They were wearing white
> robes and were holding palm branches in
> their hands. And they cried out in a loud
> voice: "Salvation belongs to our God, who
> sits on the throne, and to the Lamb." (Rev.
> 7:9, 10)

This scene sets the stage for Christ to bestow
Heaven's treasures. At the *Bema*, our Lord will
hear of our lives.

> For we must all appear before the judgment
> seat of Christ, that each one may receive
> what is due him for the things done while in
> the body, whether good or bad. Since, then,
> we know what it is to fear the Lord, we try to
> persuade men. What we are is plain to God,
> and I hope it is also plain to your conscience.
> (2 Cor. 5:10, 11)

Paul sought to persuade us. He stated there
are two things we know: We are plain to God (an
open book), and we know what it is to fear God
(which is to have a deep and profound respect
for God and His justice). Thus, we should have a
deep and profound respect for that future day
when we shall receive Heaven's treasures.

In this context, Paul referenced "good" and "bad" actions "while done in the body." Good things refer to actions of the heart that are worthy of admiration. Bad things express a lack of moral character, unbecoming for someone who claims to represent the Son of God. Our Lord is not unrighteous to forget what has been accomplished "in the [physical] body." At the *Bema*, we shall give an account of our lives. Paul said:

> For we shall all stand before the judgment seat of Christ. For it is written: "As I live, says the Lord, Every knee shall bow to Me, And every tongue shall confess to God." So then each of us shall give account of himself to God. (Rom. 14:10–12)

All in the kingdom will give a report back to God. We all will be judged based on how we built upon the foundation: the living words of our living Lord. Paul made direct reference to our foundation, Jesus Christ, and how our works will be tested by fire.

> For no one can lay any foundation other than the one already laid, which is Jesus Christ. If any man builds on this foundation using gold, silver, costly stones, wood, hay or straw, his work will be shown for what it is, because the Day will bring it to light. It will be revealed with fire, and the fire will test the quality of each man's work. If what he

has built survives, he will receive his reward. If it is burned up, he will suffer loss; he himself will be saved, but only as one escaping through the flames. (1 Cor. 3:11–15)

When we stand before our Lord, the cleansing fire of judgment will reveal the very essence of who we are. Our works will either stand the test of His assessment or they will not.

"Wood, hay or straw" represent works that will be burned up, while "gold, silver, [or] costly stones" represent works that will yield treasure. On the "Day" we stand before the Judgment Seat, everything will depend on how we built upon the foundation of Christ in this life.

During Jesus' earthly ministry, He made direct reference to building on His words:

[E]veryone who hears these words of mine and puts them into practice is like a wise man who built his house on the rock. The rain came down, the streams rose, and the winds blew and beat against that house; yet it did not fall, because it had its foundation on the rock. But everyone who hears these words of mine and does not put them into practice is like a foolish man who built his house on sand. The rain came down, the streams rose, and the winds blew and beat against that house, and it fell with a great crash. (Matt. 7:24–27)

This parable teaches wisdom. No one is

exempt from storms in life, but to those who build on the rock, Jesus Christ, a promise is given: You will still stand after the storm.

Personally, I know it's true. Life is like a live play. We are the characters. Our script is Scripture. God has already determined The End: overwhelming, joyous, eternal victory with Christ. Today, we read and act on the Scriptures. By living according to God's script, we add spiritual value to the living house of God, and store up treasures.

Look at how Peter described our lives:

> As you come to him, the living Stone—rejected by men but chosen by God and precious to him—you also, like living stones, are being built into a spiritual house to be a holy priesthood, offering spiritual sacrifices acceptable to God through Jesus Christ. (1 Peter 2:4, 5)

Those in the kingdom are "like living stones" of a "spiritual house." We adorn God's house with "gold, silver, [or] costly stones"—which are our good works, our sacrifices.

The coming time of the *Bema* is in reality a day of exchange involving works and glory. Our lives shared on Earth (in good works) will one day be expressed as our sacrifice. Our Lord, accepting that sacrifice, gives what He can give in return: Heaven's treasures.

In Revelation, our Lord provided a very specific, future treasure.

And he who overcomes, and keeps My works until the end, to him I will give power over the nations— 'He shall rule them with a rod of iron; They shall be dashed to pieces like the potter's vessels'—as I also have received from My Father; and I will give him the morning star. (Rev. 2:26–28)

Christ directed this prophecy to His kingdom (those who overcome). Yet, He earmarked this prophecy for a unique selection of those in His kingdom: those who keep His "works unto the end." To be faithful to your last breath is to store up treasures in Heaven.

With Christ's revelation about future treasure (power in the kingdom), an unmistakable picture emerges. There is a divine succession of eternal rewards: Just as the Father handed the Son divine glory, so shall the Son hand divine glory to His kingdom.

Let the King say of you: "Well done my good servant" (Luke 19:17).

Unconditional Salvation

The very reason those in the kingdom stand before Christ is because each one was saved: "Salvation belongs to our God, who sits on the throne, and to the Lamb." This shall be our cry of triumph at the *Bema*. That is John's record.

Paul prophesied of the same truth—eternal

salvation—when he spoke of the *Bema*. Unlike works which can be burned up, causing a loss of treasure, Paul revealed that salvation cannot be burned up.

Paul prophesied: "If what he has built survives, he will receive his reward. If it is burned up, he will suffer loss [loss of treasure]; he himself will be saved [salvation remains intact], but only as one escaping through the flames [of judgment]."

Like a man escaping from a burning house, losing all of his possessions (or rewards), he escapes with his life. Christ pulls him out of the flames (of judgment). At the *Bema*, he escapes with his eternal life, because salvation had come by the work of Jesus.

Even if all our works are so poor that they are all burned up at the *Bema*, the one work of Jesus—dying on the Cross—will never be burned up. If the gift of salvation is not burned up under any condition, then the gift of salvation must be unconditional.

The *Bema* ushers in the fulfillment of prophecy. If we look for the fulfillment of prophecy, then we find the truth: Salvation is an eternal gift and eternal treasures are within our grasp.

The Day of the *Bema*

When Paul prophesied of the *Bema*, he said: "The Day will bring it to light" (1 Cor. 3:13). As defined by Paul earlier in his letter, this "Day" (of the *Bema*) is "the day of the Lord Jesus Christ" (1 Cor. 1:8).

In his letter, Paul wrote to Christ's kingdom, "to those sanctified in Christ Jesus" (1 Cor. 1:2). And all who are sanctified will be judged "blameless in the day of our Lord Jesus Christ" (1 Cor. 1:8). "Blameless" literally means "not accused, with nothing laid to one's charge."[16]

> Who will bring any charge against those whom God has chosen? It is God who justifies. (Rom. 8:33)

This is the Good News of the gospel! Undeniable, irrefutable hope is granted to those in the kingdom. At the *Bema*, we will stand blameless because we have His righteousness.

> Now to Him Who is able to keep you without stumbling or slipping or falling, and to present [you] unblemished (blameless and faultless) before the presence of His glory in triumphant joy and exultation [with unspeakable, ecstatic delight]. (Jude 24)

Commit your works to the Lord, And your thoughts will be established. (Prov. 16:3)

6

Treasures: Our Inheritance

The Spirit Himself [thus] testifies together with our own spirit, [assuring us] that we are children of God. And if we are [His] children, then we are [His] heirs also: heirs of God and fellow heirs with Christ [sharing His inheritance with Him].
—The Apostle Paul (Rom. 8:16, 17)

S alvation is not the only gift that is unconditional. So is the inheritance.

Paul revealed the connection between salvation (being a child of God), and the inheritance (being an heir of God). The Spirit of Christ transforms us into children of God, and if we are His children, then we automatically are fellow heirs with Christ and heirs of God. Thus, the treasures of the inheritance are not earned, but granted.

As Christ gave revelation about our crowns to James, Paul, Peter, and John, so He did with the inheritance. Enjoy their prophecies.

James prophesied:

Listen, my dear brothers: Has not God chosen those who are poor in the eyes of the world to be rich in faith and to inherit the kingdom he promised those who love him? (James 2:5)

Paul prophesied:

Giving thanks to the Father, Who has qualified and made us fit to share the portion which is the inheritance of the saints (God's holy people) in the Light. [The Father] has delivered and drawn us to Himself out of the control and the dominion of darkness and has transferred us into the kingdom of the Son of His love. (Col. 1:12, 13)

Peter prophesied:

Praise to God for a Living Hope: Praise be to the God and Father of our Lord Jesus Christ! In his great mercy he has given us new birth into a living hope through the resurrection of Jesus Christ from the dead, and into an inheritance that can never perish, spoil or fade—kept in heaven for you, who through faith are shielded by God's power until the coming of the salvation that is ready to be revealed in the last time. (1 Peter 1:3–5)

Consider this: If "through faith [you] are

shielded by God's power until the coming of the salvation that is ready to be revealed in the last time," then how can anything affect your salvation? It cannot.

Consider this: If you have a "new birth" into "an inheritance that can never perish, spoil or fade—kept in heaven for you," then how can anything affect your inheritance? It cannot.

The new birth is a gift from God. The "measure of faith" (Rom. 12:3) is a gift from God. The inheritance is a gift from God.

It was during His Sermon on the Mount, that Jesus introduced us to our inheritance: "Blessed are the meek: for they shall inherit the earth" (Matt. 5:5). In Revelation, our King unfolded revelation never before revealed about our coming paradise, our inheritance.

The New Heaven and New Earth

To John, Christ gave the following vision of the coming creation:

Then I saw a new heaven and a new earth, for the former heaven and the former earth had passed away, and the sea was no more. (Rev. 21:1)

I saw the Holy City, the new Jerusalem, coming down out of heaven from God, prepared as a bride beautifully dressed for her husband. And I heard a loud voice from the throne saying, "Now the dwelling of God is with men, and he will live with them. They will be his people, and God himself will be with them and be their God. He will wipe every tear from their eyes. There will be no more death or mourning or crying or pain, for the old order of things has passed away." He who was seated on the throne said, "I am making everything new!" Then he said, "Write this down, for these words are trustworthy and true." He said to me: "It is done. I am the Alpha and the Omega, the Beginning and the End. To him who is thirsty I will give to drink without cost from the spring of the water of life. He who overcomes will inherit all this, and I will be his God and he will be my son." (Rev. 21:2–7).

"He who overcomes will inherit all this, and I will be his God and he will be my son." We become a son of God and an heir of God by overcoming the world through Christ, for "everyone born of God overcomes the world. This is the victory that has overcome the world, even our faith" (1 John 5:4).

In Revelation, Christ revealed vivid details of our inheritance. He revealed eternal treasure, and to each church He said: "He who has an ear, let him hear what the Spirit says to the churches" (Rev. 3:22). May we all have ears to hear.

Our Lord prophesied:

To him that overcomes I will give to eat of the tree of life, which is in the midst of the paradise of God. (Rev. 2:7)

He that overcomes shall not be hurt by the second death. (Rev. 2:11)

To him that overcomes I will give to eat of the hidden manna and will give him a small white stone and in the stone a new name written, which no one knows except the one that receives it. (Rev. 2:17)

He that overcomes shall likewise be clothed in white raiment, and I will not blot out his name out of the book of life, but I will confess his name before my Father and before his angels. (Rev. 3:5)

He that overcomes I will make a pillar in the temple of my God, and he shall go out no more, and I will write upon him the name of my God, and the name of the city of my God which is the new Jerusalem, which comes down out of heaven from and with my God, and I will write upon him my new name. (Rev. 3:12)

To him that overcomes will I grant to sit with me in my throne, even as I also overcame and have sat down with my Father in his throne. (Rev. 3:21)

These eternal treasures cannot be completely comprehended any more than the fullness of the coming world can be comprehended. "No eye has seen, no ear has heard, no mind has conceived what God has prepared for those who love him" (1 Cor. 2:9).

Yet we do know this: Those who overcome will have a new name, a white stone, hidden manna, will be dressed in white, will be acknowledged before the Father and His angels, and upon those in the kingdom the King will write three names: the name of God, the name of the city of God, and Christ's new name.

None will be hurt by the second death. This is the death suffered by the unrighteous at the Great White Throne. There is no impact on the King's kingdom. (See the Epilogue.)

Finally, none in the kingdom will be blotted out of the "book of life" (which catalogs our righteous works). When Paul spoke of this book, he referred to his "co-workers, whose names are in the book of life" (Phil. 4:3). (King David also spoke of the book of life in the context of works.[17])

The assurance given to John is that none in the King's kingdom will ever be blotted out of the book of life. This assurance is part of the inheritance.

In Revelation, John added another treasure of our inheritance, and he spoke of another book: the Lamb's book of life. All who are in the Lamb's book of life will inherit the right to enter the gates of new Jerusalem.

> And he carried me [John] away in the Spirit to a mountain great and high, and showed me the Holy City, Jerusalem, coming down out of heaven from God. The twelve gates were twelve pearls, each gate made of a single pearl. The great street of the city was of gold, as pure as transparent glass. It had a great, high wall with twelve gates, and with twelve angels at the gates. I did not see a temple in the city, because the Lord God Almighty and the Lamb are its temple. The city does not need the sun or the moon to shine on it, for the glory of God gives it light, and the Lamb is its lamp. The nations will walk by its light, and the kings of the earth will bring their splendor into it. On no day will its gates ever be shut, for there will be no night there. The glory and honor of the nations will be brought into it. Nothing impure will ever enter it, nor will anyone who does what is shameful or deceitful, but only those whose names are written in the Lamb's book of life. (Rev. 21:10–12, 21–27)

> Blessed are those who wash their robes, that they may have the right to the tree of life and may go through the gates into the city [new Jerusalem]. (Rev. 22:14)

When John spoke of the inheritance, he prophesied of the Lamb's book and new

Jerusalem in the same breath. He said: "Nothing impure will ever enter it [new Jerusalem], but only those whose names are written in the Lamb's book of life." He also said: "Blessed are those who wash their robes that they may go through the gates into the city."

If those who wash their robes go through the gates of the city, and only those written in the Lamb's book of life enter the city, then those who are in the Lamb's book washed their robes (in His blood).

In essence, the Lamb's book of life refers to grace. By grace we are saved; we washed our robes in the blood of the Lamb. Thus, we are in the Lamb's book of life by *His* work on the Cross. In contrast, the book of life remembers *our* works.

Christ's kingdom will be forever etched on the pages of each book. Those in the books are sealed by the Spirit, and the inheritance is guaranteed.

To summarize, all in the King's kingdom will inherit:

Eternal Life
Eternal Earth
Eternal Kingdom
Eternal Jerusalem
Eternal Treasure

God grants all this because His Son, "is the Mediator and Negotiator of a new covenant [that is, an entirely new agreement uniting

God and man], so that those who have been called [by God] may receive [the fulfillment of] the promised eternal inheritance." (Heb. 9:15)

The house of the righteous contains great treasure, but the income of the wicked brings ruin. (Prov. 15:6)

ACT THREE

7

In the Beginning

[W]e speak of God's secret wisdom, a wisdom that has been hidden and that God destined for our glory before time began. None of the rulers of this age understood it, for if they had, they would not have crucified the Lord of glory.

—The Apostle Paul (1 Cor. 2:7, 8)

In the beginning, when God brought forth creation, evil was unknown. The Creator created angelic beings and human beings (among other creations). Spirit beings would inhabit the heavens, and human beings would inhabit the Earth. When the Creator brought forth the angel Lucifer, God anointed him as a guardian cherub. On Earth, God brought forth another type of creation: flesh and blood. Humankind would reflect its Creator in the physical realm, just as Lucifer had in the spiritual realm.

God is holy and righteous, and that's how He created His creation. Free will, given by God, would enable the Father to coexist with His independent "intelligence." With that free will, however, came active rebellion against the Creator, resulting in a loss of harmony within both the heavenly and the earthly realms.

Whereas Lucifer sought to usurp the throne of God, Adam and Eve succumbed to deception in the Garden of Eden. Unholy created beings then existed within creation, and spiritual warfare raged against the Creator. Lucifer's expressed intent was to displace God and ascend to His throne.

However, the guardian cherub overestimated the value of his initiative. The progress of dark spiritual power would be reversed by way of flesh and blood; it would come in the form of God's only begotten Son, Jesus Christ. The Father purposed that through the planned death of Jesus, souls upon Earth could be liberated from mortality.

Through His Son, the Creator would outwit Lucifer and finally bring an end to evil and death. The fallen angel never would have crucified the Messiah had he known the consequences.

History and Prophecy

Lucifer is the name that God gave to His angelic model of perfection. Created as a magnificent angel, Lucifer was with God on the holy mount, the pinnacle of the heavens. The guardian cherub walked faultlessly in all of his ways until evil was conceived within. Lucifer became obsessed with what was reserved for God: worship. Therewith, the angel of light turned to darkness:

> You were the model of perfection, full of wisdom and perfect in beauty. You were in Eden, the garden of God; every precious stone adorned you. You were anointed as a guardian cherub, for so I ordained you. You were on the holy mount of God; you walked among the fiery stones. You were blameless in your ways from the day you were created till wickedness was found in you. So I drove you in disgrace from the mount of God, and I expelled you, O guardian cherub, from among the fiery stones. Your heart became proud on account of your beauty, and you corrupted your wisdom because of your splendor. (Ezek. 28:12–17)

> How you are fallen from heaven, O Lucifer, son of the morning! How you are cut down to the ground, You who weakened the nations! For you have said in your heart: "I will ascend into heaven, I will exalt my throne above the stars of God; I will also sit on the mount of the congregation On the farthest sides of the north; I will ascend above the heights of the clouds, I will be like the Most High." (Isa. 14:12–14)

The former guardian cherub spoke his prophecy into the ears of God: The throne of

Heaven would be his. He would be like the Most High.

By his own power, Lucifer transformed himself into the highest-ranking dark angel: Satan. The son of the dawn became the angel of darkness. Pride extinguished divine light, and wisdom was corrupted. Now, the fallen angel would rule his own kingdom, having ultimate command over one third of the angels (those who rejected God with Lucifer (Rev. 12:3, 4)).

With his spiritual power, Satan would tempt mankind to commit treason against God. Thus, the fallen angel would divide Heaven and Earth. Sin brought mortality, and with that, God would be separated from His mortal creation. The fallen angel would cause this calamity by initiating a rebellion upon Earth by deception.

Satan knew the prophecy that God had given in the Garden of Eden, that Adam and Eve did not have the right to distort the standard of truth regarding good and evil. Satan would claim the opposite; the fallen angel would give man the false sense of security that he could be as a god. But the true God had already told Adam that he would surely die if he ate of that "fruit":

> The Lord God commanded the man, "You are free to eat from any tree in the garden; but you must not eat from the tree of the knowledge of good and evil, for when you eat of it you will surely die." (Gen. 2:16, 17)

By man's eating the fruit, human creation

would no longer be in harmony with the Creator. Partaking of the tree would be much more than innocent self-interest; it would be an act of defiance, and by doing so, Adam and Eve would determine for themselves what is good and what is evil. Satan became fixated on bringing this to pass.

On the day Satan appeared as an angel of light (the serpent), he spoke beautifully about the "deadly" tree.

> Now the serpent was craftier than any of the wild animals the Lord God had made. He said to the woman, "Did God really say, 'You must not eat from any tree in the garden'?" The woman said to the serpent, "We may eat fruit from the trees in the garden, but God did say, 'You must not eat fruit from the tree that is in the middle of the garden, and you must not touch it, or you will die.'" "You will not surely die," the serpent said to the woman. "For God knows that when you eat of it your eyes will be opened, and you will be like God, knowing good and evil." When the woman saw that the fruit of the tree was good for food and pleasing to the eye, and also desirable for gaining wisdom, she took some and ate it. She also gave some to her husband, who was with her, and he ate it. Then the eyes of both of them were opened, and they realized they were naked; so they sewed fig leaves together and made coverings for themselves. (Gen. 3:1–7)

In desiring to be as God, Adam and Eve broke from God. Once their eyes were opened to this fact, the two realized that they were no longer covered by God's righteousness. They now saw their flesh and blood as sinful.

In Eden, Satan accused God of deliberately denying Adam and Eve from attaining an advanced state. He claimed that God was keeping them from becoming gods. Eve believed Satan.

Ironically, Satan was correct about the eyes of man being opened, but instead of becoming gods, Adam and Eve realized their reduced stature in creation. The prophecy from God was true and the ramifications were soon to follow.

> Then the man and his wife heard the sound of the Lord God as he was walking in the garden in the cool of the day, and they hid from the Lord God among the trees of the garden. But the Lord God called to the man, "Where are you?"
>
> He answered, "I heard you in the garden, and I was afraid because I was naked; so I hid."
>
> And he said, "Who told you that you were naked? Have you eaten from the tree that I commanded you not to eat from?"
>
> The man said, "The woman you put here with me—she gave me some fruit from the tree, and I ate it. Then the Lord God said to the woman, "What is this you have done?"

The woman said, "The serpent deceived me, and I ate." (Gen. 3:8–13)

Righteousness was lost in Eden. Therefore, Adam feared God and hid from Him. As sin had caused a separation between man and his Creator, paradise would now come to an abrupt halt.

Satan had beguiled man into desiring what he himself had succumbed to: the desire to be as God. With this act, humankind could no longer have access to the tree of life.

And the Lord God said, "The man has now become like one of us, knowing good and evil. He must not be allowed to reach out his hand and take also from the tree of life and eat, and live forever." So the Lord God banished him from the Garden of Eden to work the ground from which he had been taken. (Gen. 3:22, 23)

Now denied access to the tree, unholy man was separated from the divine. In a moment of time, Adam became mortal. The Creator could not allow sinful man to live forever in Eden, because that would have yielded permanent disharmony in creation.

Despite the separation, God promised that He would reverse the consequences facing the offspring of Adam and Eve. He prophesied that a Savior would be sent to release man from the slavery of mortality. Simultaneously, the Lord

God condemned Satan for his treachery:

> So the Lord God said to the serpent, "Because you have done this, Cursed are you above all the livestock and all the wild animals! You will crawl on your belly and you will eat dust all the days of your life. And I will put enmity between you and the woman [Eve], and between your offspring and hers; he [Christ] will crush your head." (Gen. 3:14, 15)

The prophecy from God was that His Son would crush the hope of darkness. Never would the fallen angel recover from the wound that Christ would inflict. What Lucifer had initiated, God would finish. God Himself prophesied Satan's fate:

> [Y]ou shall be brought down to Sheol (Hades), to the innermost recesses of the pit (the region of the dead). (Isa. 14:15)

> I will bring forth a fire from the midst of thee, it shall devour thee, and I will bring thee to ashes upon the earth in the sight of all them that behold thee and never shalt thou be any more. (Ezek. 28:18, 19)

God decreed Satan's fate: ashes. Yet the fallen angel intended to defeat this prophecy; he would refute God by inspiring religious authorities to crucify the Christ, the Messiah, the anointed one of God.

The fallen angel would bring an end to Jesus through the false religious leaders in Jerusalem known as the Pharisees. These counterfeit temple priests would participate in the conspiracy to kill Jesus of Nazareth, for His life threatened their very existence.

> Then the chief priests and the Pharisees called a meeting of the Sanhedrin [high court]. "What are we accomplishing?" they asked. "Here is this man [Jesus] performing many miraculous signs. If we let him go on like this, everyone will believe in him, and then the Romans will come and take away both our place and our nation." Then one of them, named Caiaphas, who was high priest that year, spoke up, "You know nothing at all! You do not realize that it is better for you that one man die for the people than that the whole nation perish." He did not say this on his own, but as high priest that year he prophesied that Jesus would die for the Jewish nation. So from that day on they plotted to take his life. (John 11:47–51, 53)

The Pharisees were concerned about their place in Israel and potentially losing the entire country to the Romans. Jesus had to die if both were to be saved. Hence, the fulfillment of Satan's purpose would come by way of flesh and blood.

This conflict in Jerusalem was the flash

point between two spiritual powers. Whereas evil manifested itself through the Pharisees, the divine power of God manifested itself through Jesus. In Christ's verbal exchange with His adversaries, He disclosed their hypocrisy and identified their true nature.

> As it is, you are determined to kill me, a man who has told you the truth that I heard from God. You are doing the things your own father does. If God were your Father, you would love me, for I came from God and now am here. I have not come on my own; but he sent me. You belong to your father, the devil, and you want to carry out your father's desire. He was a murderer from the beginning, not holding to the truth, for there is no truth in him. When he lies, he speaks his native language, for he is a liar and the father of lies. (John 8:40–42, 44)

The fallen angel had darkened the minds of those who sat upon the seat of religious authority. Their souls belonged to darkness, sealed shut by the seed of Satan.

The Pharisees' perception of reality demanded the death of Earth's Messiah. Therein, the children of darkness would fulfill the will of their father; they would falsely accuse Jesus of blasphemy against God to carry out their own agenda.

> The high priest said to him, "I charge you

under oath by the living God: Tell us if you are the Christ, the Son of God." "Yes, it is as you say," Jesus replied. "But I say to all of you: In the future you will see the Son of Man sitting at the right hand of the Mighty One and coming on the clouds of heaven." Then the high priest tore his clothes and said, "He has spoken blasphemy! Why do we need any more witnesses? Look, now you have heard the blasphemy. What do you think?" "He is worthy of death," they answered. (Matt. 26:63–66)

Accused of blasphemy, Jesus would face Crucifixion. Therein, the dark angel believed that he would stop the kingdom of God through Jesus' death, blotting out the light sent by Heaven.

In reality, the fallen angel participated in giving mankind the ultimate sacrifice for sin—the Pharisees slew God's Lamb. "Christ, our Passover lamb, has been sacrificed" (1 Cor. 5:7). Just as the Passover lamb in Egypt saved Israelites from death, so the Lamb of God would save souls from mortality. Jesus sacrificed His own life so that others could live eternally. With His Resurrection, He offered Himself to the Father in Heaven as the ultimate atonement for sin.

For Christ did not enter a man-made sanctuary that was only a copy of the true one; he entered heaven itself, now to appear for us in God's presence. [H]e has appeared once for all at the end of the ages to do away with sin by the sacrifice of himself. (Heb. 9:24, 26)

Jesus' sacrifice did "away with sin" and its consequences. He did not receive the sinful nature that Adam had passed on to humankind because God was His Father. Therefore, He was in a position to live a sinless life and die as God's gift to man. Hence, any person who accepts this sacrifice is granted eternal life.

Satan lost his trump card over man because mortality was permanently affected. Christ "destroyed" the dark angel by nullifying his power over death: "By his [Jesus'] death he might destroy him who holds the power of death—that is, the devil—and free those who all their lives were held in slavery by their fear of death" (Heb. 2:14, 15).

Freedom from the fear of death is central to Christ's gospel. Eternal life for human souls was not what Satan had envisioned when Jesus bled on the Cross. Preoccupied with Jesus' death, the fallen angel could not foresee the ramifications of his actions.

With the Crucifixion, Resurrection, and Ascension, all bloodlines now had an advocate—Jesus Christ—in the presence of God. The Son of God became man's mediator: "For there is one God and one mediator between God and mankind, the man Christ Jesus, who gave himself as a ransom for all people" (1 Tim. 2:5,

6). Christ was placed in a position to release souls from death and grant eternal life for all who overcome deception and reach out to God through Him.

> Therefore he is able to save completely those who come to God through him, because he always lives to intercede for them. We do have such a high priest, who sat down at the right hand of the throne of the Majesty in heaven, and who serves in the sanctuary, the true tabernacle set up by the Lord, not by man. (Heb. 7:25; 8:1, 2)

Situated in the true tabernacle in Heaven, man's great high priest was positioned to intercede in the lives of souls upon Earth. Through the Messiah, man would finally be empowered to exit the death sentence passed on from Adam.

> Therefore, just as sin entered the world through one man [Adam], and death through sin, and in this way death came to all men. For if the many died by the trespass of the one man, how much more did God's grace and the gift that came by the grace of the one man, Jesus Christ, overflow to the many! (Rom. 5:12, 15)

> For since death came through a man, the resurrection of the dead comes also through a man. For as in Adam all die, so in Christ all

will be made alive. But each in his own turn:
Christ, the first-fruits; then, when he comes,
those who belong to him. (1 Cor. 15:21–23)

Christ was the "first-fruits" from the dead,
and those who belong to Him shall also be made
alive when He returns from Heaven.

Ultimately, the destiny of all souls lies with
God or Satan. Earthly inhabitants have free will
to embrace divine light or reject it.

The fallen angel wields the power of death
by inducing the false pleasure of rejecting God.
Satan lures his prey away from the truth and
into a life void of meaning. Thereby, darkened
minds feed upon thoughts of spiritual deception.
Empty words are served by the voice of demonic
power; all the lies that discredit the light of
Heaven pour forth to twist human logic. The
foundational fallacy promoted by Satan is that
mankind can gain some greater reward on this
Earth. However, as Christ proclaimed: "What
good is it for a man to gain the whole world, yet
forfeit his soul?" (Mark 8:36).

The lie is to live in this world as if there is
nothing to lose. The question asked by the Son of
God was to weigh the alternative. According to
Christ, there is something to lose: the soul. The
soul is the life that springs from the seed passed
on from Adam. "For the [soul] life of the flesh is
in the blood" (Lev.17:11).

In humankind, there exists a distinction
between souls. If the soul is not forfeited, it will
live eternally. In contrast, if the soul is ruined, it

can never regenerate itself. That is why Christ forewarned the world of Satan's power: "Do not be afraid of those who kill the body but cannot kill the soul. Rather, be afraid of the One [Satan] who can destroy both soul and body in hell" (Matt. 10:28). "Hell," spoken here by Jesus, is the future funeral pyre—the "devouring judgment fire" (Greek: *Gehenna*[18]).

Satan, who is the god of this age, destroys the mind, and thereby the soul, by a web of lies, for his distortion causes unbelief: "The god of this age has blinded the minds of unbelievers, so that they cannot see the light of the gospel of the glory of Christ, who is the image of God" (2 Cor. 4:4). Those who are blinded by Satan cannot see the darkness that pulses in the airwaves of life because they are in the midst of it.

Without God's revelation and Holy Spirit, the spiritual dimension upon Earth remains misunderstood: "The man without the Spirit does not accept the things that come from the Spirit of God, for they are foolishness to him, and he cannot understand them, because they are spiritually discerned" (1 Cor. 2:14).

In the Holy Land, Jesus said, "You will know the truth, and the truth will set you free" (John 8:32). Freedom means no longer being a slave to spiritual darkness and its consequences. In the spiritual war fought upon Earth, truth is the key to alter the fate of the soul: "Let him know that he who turns a sinner from the error of his way will save a soul from death and cover a multitude of sins" (James 5:20). A saved soul, filled with the Holy Spirit, means triumph over death and Satan, and thus: "The one who is in you [Christ] is greater than the one who is in the world [Satan]" (1 John 4:4).

God "desires all men to be saved and to come to the knowledge of the truth" (1 Tim. 2:4). The Lord God said: "As surely as I live, declares the Sovereign Lord, I take no pleasure in the death of the wicked, but rather that they turn from their ways and live" (Ezek. 33:11). God's invitation to Earth is to embrace His Son. When the door is opened to Christ, eternity unfolds.

Almighty God did not bring forth this creation in vain. With it, the Father will fulfill His plan to live with His sons without the presence of darkness. The invisible Creator has fully disclosed His strategy in written form, and Satan is powerless to alter the future. The battle plans are already drawn, and the outcome is without doubt. Souls will be saved from death because the Messiah won the right to ransom them from the power of the grave. In this spiritual conflict for the soul, our Creator claims victory when Satan loses a human soul to eternity.

Now, listen to the apostle Paul reveal the eternal relationship we have with our Lord:

> Who shall separate us from the love of Christ? Shall tribulation, or distress, or persecution, or famine, or nakedness, or peril, or sword? Nay, in all these things we are more than conquerors through Him that

loved us. For I am persuaded that neither death, nor life, nor angels, nor principalities, nor powers, nor things present, nor things to come, nor height, nor depth, nor any other creature, shall be able to separate us from the love of God which is in Christ Jesus our Lord. (Rom. 8:35, 37–39)

My son, do not forget my law, but let your heart keep my commands; for length of days and long life and peace they will add to you. (Prov. 3:1, 2)

8

Treasure: The Mystery

My goal is that they may be encouraged in heart and united in love, so that they may have the full riches of complete understanding, in order that they may know the mystery of God, namely, Christ, in whom are hidden all the treasures of wisdom and knowledge.

—The Apostle Paul (Col. 2:2, 3)

I n Old Testament times, the stone temple in Jerusalem was the focus of communion with man and God. This, however, foreshadowed God's ultimate plan: a temple made of people, filled with the Holy Spirit. God's communion with man would be by way of a spiritual temple, which would encompass the globe and have no earthly boundaries. With the New Testament, the apostles revealed the glorious understanding of God's plan: to save us, to live within us, and to dwell among us in His living temple. Paul said:

For we are the temple of the living God. As

God has said: "I will live with them and walk among them, and I will be their God, and they will be my people." (2 Cor. 6:16)

All who are born of God are born into the temple of the living God. When Paul said, "For we are the temple of the living God," he quoted God's own prophecy to explain it. For, in the days of Moses, God Himself prophesied: "I will live with them and walk among them, and I will be their God, and they will be my people" (Lev. 26:12). God foresaw the day when He would establish a global temple, filled with His people, born of the Holy Spirit. Thus, He would live with us, walk among us, be our God, and we would be His people. Yet, when God issued His prophecy, only He knew the true meaning of it—that it would lead to the living temple.

It wasn't until the days of the New Testament, and the revelation given by Christ to Paul, that the hidden wisdom of God was fully revealed. Paul said:

For I want you to know, brethren, that the Gospel which was proclaimed and made known by me is not man's gospel [a human invention, according to or patterned after any human standard]. For indeed I did not receive it from man, nor was I taught it, but [it came to me] through a [direct] revelation [given] by Jesus Christ (the Messiah)." (Gal. 1:11, 12)

The Son of God taught Paul the mystery, which included the creation of the living temple. And Paul said his desire for us was that we "may know the mystery of God, namely, Christ, in whom are hidden all the treasures of wisdom and knowledge" (Col. 2:2, 3). The mystery, once hidden in Christ, is revealed to those who seek "the way, the truth, and the life" (John 14:6). Those who embrace the Messiah are granted access to the inner chamber of knowledge: the mystery of the living temple.

The Temple of the Living God

Paul and Peter both described the King's kingdom as the temple of the living God:

> For through him we both have access to the Father by one Spirit. Consequently, you are no longer foreigners and strangers, but fellow citizens with God's people and also members of his household, built on the foundation of the apostles and prophets, with Christ Jesus himself as the chief cornerstone. In him the whole building is joined together and rises to become a holy temple in the Lord. And in him you too are being built together to become a dwelling in which God lives by his Spirit. (Eph. 2:18–22)

> As you come to him, the living Stone, rejected by humans but chosen by God and

precious to him, you also, like living stones, are being built into a spiritual house to be a holy priesthood, offering spiritual sacrifices acceptable to God through Jesus Christ. For in Scripture it says: "See, I lay a stone in Zion, a chosen and precious cornerstone, and the one who trusts in him will never be put to shame." Now to you who believe, this stone is precious. (1 Peter 2:4–7)

As Christ is the chief cornerstone, the whole building is designed around and upon Him. His words comprise the foundation on which the living stones are built.

By way of His Son, God created a new, global, eternal kingdom—a living temple—with His Son as King and great high priest.

Therefore, since we have a great high priest who has ascended into heaven, Jesus the Son of God, let us hold firmly to the faith we profess. (Heb. 4:14)

Our high priest of the living temple is our mediator, who is our advocate with the Father. "For there is only one God and likewise only one mediator between God and men, the man Christ Jesus" (1 Tim. 2:5). "My dear children, I write this to you so that you will not sin. But if anybody does sin, we have an advocate with the Father—Jesus Christ, the Righteous One" (1 John 2:1). If in our walk with God in the temple we find ourselves being at cross purposes with

God (we sin), we always have an advocate with the Father: our Lord and Savior.

The Son of God ascended to the right hand of God and there He reigns as great high priest over His global temple. He intercedes for us. That's His role. And our role is this: We are all "priests" (Rev. 1:6) in a "royal priesthood" (1 Peter 2:9), where each believer offers his or her life as a "living sacrifice" (Rom. 12:1).

This revelation of the living temple did not exist during Jesus' earthly ministry. That is why the revelation of this mystery is found not in the Gospels, but in the letters of Paul, Peter, and John. In Paul's first letter to the Corinthians, he revealed the wisdom God hid from His enemies, and from His own prophets—which enabled His plan of the living temple to come to pass.

[W]e speak of God's secret wisdom, a wisdom that has been hidden and that God destined for our glory before time began. None of the rulers of this age understood it, for if they had, they would not have crucified the Lord of glory. (1 Cor. 2:7, 8)

There never would have been a living temple, and Satan's henchmen never would have crucified Jesus—had they known what you are about to read.

The Holy Days

The physical temple of stone (in the Old Testament) foreshadowed the spiritual, living temple of Christ (in the New Testament). And the physical celebrations of the holy days in the stone temple foreshadowed the spiritual celebrations of what the Lamb of God would accomplish (creating the living temple).

God's enemies failed to grasp that the holy days celebrated by the Israelites in the physical temple were in actuality "rehearsals" that foreshadowed what the Lamb of God would achieve with His personal presence.

This is what the princes of the world (working for the power of darkness) didn't understand: "The law is only a shadow of the good things that are coming" (Heb. 10:1). Satan saw the Israelites celebrate the holy days in the temple, but he was clueless as to their real significance, for those celebrations foreshadowed Christ's accomplishments on the very holy days.

Holy days are known as "feasts of the Lord" (Lev. 23:2). A feast (Hebrew: *Moed*[19]) means a festival that has an "appointed time." It also means a festival that is a "signal" for what is appointed beforehand (by God). In other words, these holy days were not only physical celebrations; they foreshadowed (signaled) what God had in mind about what the Messiah would accomplish for us by the following: His death,

His burial, His Resurrection, and His baptizing of the apostles with Holy Spirit.

These four events correspond to the first four holy days (the spring holy days). With His first coming, the Messiah fulfilled them: Jesus, the "Lamb of God" (John 1:29), was sacrificed on Passover. He was in the burial tomb on the Feast of Unleavened Bread; He was resurrected from the dead on the Feast of First fruits; and, finally, Christ sent the Holy Spirit to His apostles on the Feast of Weeks (Pentecost), which was 50 days after the Resurrection. These events occurred as appointed by God.

In the future, Christ's kingdom will be raptured according to the same divine timetable. The kingdom will be transported to Heaven on the fifth holy day: the Feast of Trumpets (*Rosh Hashanah*).

In the Old Testament, *Rosh Hashanah* did not have a specific day or hour assigned on the Hebrew calendar. Instead, it commenced at the sighting of the seventh new moon. During some year in the future, on the Feast of Trumpets, the King will harvest His kingdom. (See the Epilogue.)

God ordained all of this before the world unto our glory. God kept this a mystery until it was fully revealed by Christ to Paul.

It was in Paul's first letter to the Corinthians, where he said: "[W]e speak of God's secret wisdom, a wisdom that has been hidden and that God destined for our glory before time began" (1 Cor. 2:7). In this same letter, Paul revealed God's secret wisdom. Paul referenced the first five holy days, and their hidden spiritual significance: The fulfillment of the first four holy days by Jesus Christ led to the birth of the temple of the living God (the church), and the fulfillment of the fifth holy day will bring the future salvation of the church (at the appearance of Christ in the sky).

1 Corinthians: Five Holy Days

Passover

> For Christ, our Passover lamb, has been sacrificed. (1 Cor. 5:7)

The Feast of Unleavened Bread

> For whenever you eat this bread and drink this cup, you proclaim the Lord's death until he comes. (1 Cor. 11:26)

The Feast of First Fruits

> But Christ has indeed been raised from the dead, the first fruits of those who have fallen asleep. For since death came through a man, the resurrection of the dead comes also through a man. For as in Adam all die, so in

Christ all will be made alive. But each in turn: Christ, the first fruits; then, when he comes, those who belong to him. (1 Cor. 15:20–23)

The Feast of Weeks (Pentecost)

For we were all baptized by one Spirit so as to form one body—whether Jews or Gentiles, slave or free—and we were all given the one Spirit to drink. (1 Cor. 12:13)

In the law it is written, With men of other tongues and other lips will I speak unto this people. (1 Cor. 14:21)

The Feast of Trumpets

Listen, I tell you a mystery: We will not all sleep, but we will all be changed—in a flash, in the twinkling of an eye, at the last trumpet. For the trumpet will sound, the dead will be raised imperishable, and we will be changed. (1 Cor. 15:51, 52)

Is it any wonder that Paul declared the prophetic holy days in the very letter that affirms God's enemies were outwitted and defeated?

God's enemies were defeated because they didn't see the mystery. God had to keep this mystery of the coming salvation hidden even from His prophets.

> Concerning this salvation, the prophets, who spoke of the grace that was to come to you, searched intently and with the greatest care, trying to find out the time and circumstances to which the Spirit of Christ in them was pointing when he predicted the sufferings of the Messiah and the glories that would follow. (1 Peter 1:10, 11)

Looking forward, the Old Testament prophets could not "find out the time." Looking back, we know the time; it started the year Jesus offered Himself as God's sacrifice, dying on the Cross. That year marked a new beginning for mankind: The mystery of the living temple became a reality and that temple continues to this day. It's the mystery, revealed. Today, Jesus Christ reigns as our great high priest over the living temple because twenty centuries ago He fulfilled the will of God.

Jesus said: "Everything must be fulfilled that is written about me in the Law of Moses, the Prophets and the Psalms" (Luke 24:44). It is because Jesus fulfilled the Law that we are freed from the Law: "For Christ *is* the end of the law for righteousness to everyone who believes" (Rom. 10:4). We are made righteous and we are saved eternally.

Jesus became our complete salvation, which would reflect the holy days: Christ is our Passover Lamb (that cleanses sin); Christ is our bread of life (divine revelation to transform the mind); Christ is our first fruits from the dead (rescuing us from the power of death); Christ is our baptizer (baptizing us with the Holy Spirit), and Christ is our future salvation (rapturing us to His throne). All this was hidden in the holy days, which were given to Moses. (For a detailed review of God's prophetic holy days, see www.thetimeline.org.)

When God gave Moses these holy days, God also issued His prophecy: "I will live with them and walk among them, and I will be their God, and they will be my people" (Lev. 26:12). When God gave His prophecy, only He knew its true meaning and how it was connected to the holy days.

Yet, God's intention to establish a living temple was in His mind long before Moses—it was His intention to do so from before the foundation of the world. That is exactly what Christ revealed.

Christ's Revelation

Christ revealed to Paul God's plan:

Even as [in His love] He chose us [actually picked us out for Himself as His own] in Christ before the foundation of the world, that we should be holy (consecrated and set apart for Him) and blameless in His sight, even above reproach, before Him in love.

For He foreordained us (destined us, planned in love for us) to be adopted (revealed) as His own children through Jesus Christ, in accordance with the purpose of His will [because it pleased Him and was His kind intent]—[So that we might be] to the praise and the commendation of His glorious grace (favor and mercy), which He so freely bestowed on us in the Beloved. In Him we have redemption (deliverance and salvation) through His blood, the remission (forgiveness) of our offenses (shortcomings and trespasses), in accordance with the riches *and* the generosity of His gracious favor, Which He lavished upon us in every kind of wisdom and understanding (practical insight and prudence), Making known to us the mystery (secret) of His will (of His plan, of His purpose). (Eph. 1:4–9)

These treasures of wisdom and knowledge, once a mystery hidden in Christ, are ours to understand—and revel in for eternity. We are God's people, and He is our God.

We are one in Christ Jesus. There is no longer a separation between Jew and Gentile, or between bloodlines, or between any other man-made class system. All believers are priests in the living temple, members of the kingdom of Christ, each with their own unique role to fulfill in the body of Christ. All believers partake of the Good News—which includes the hope of glory: the Rapture and all that follows.

This is the revelation our Lord gave to Paul:

[B]y [divine] revelation the mystery was made known to me [Paul], as I have already written in brief. By referring to this, when you read it you can understand my insight into the mystery of Christ, which in other generations was not disclosed to mankind, as it has now been revealed to His holy apostles and prophets by the [Holy] Spirit; [it is this:] that the Gentiles are now joint heirs [with the Jews] and members of the same body, and joint partakers [sharing] in the [same divine] promise in Christ Jesus through [their faith in] the good news [of salvation]. (Eph. 3:3–6)

[T]he mystery which hath been hid from ages and from generations, but now is made manifest to his saints: to whom God would make known what is the riches of the glory of this mystery among the Gentiles; which is Christ in you, the hope of glory. (Col. 1:26, 27)

The fear [reverence] of the Lord is the beginning of wisdom, and knowledge of the Holy One is understanding. (Prov. 9:10)

9

Treasure in Earthen Vessels

For God, who said, "Let light shine out of darkness," is the One who has shone in our hearts to give us the Light of the knowledge of the glory and majesty of God [clearly revealed] in the face of Christ. But we have this precious treasure [the good news about salvation] in [unworthy] earthen vessels [of human frailty], so that the grandeur and surpassing greatness of the power will be [shown to be] from God [His sufficiency] and not from ourselves.

—The Apostle Paul (2 Cor. 4:6, 7)

During His time in the Holy Land, Jesus introduced us to the concept of worshipping God in the Spirit and in truth. No longer would the temple in Jerusalem be the focus of worship, but rather, worship would be in the temple of the living God. Jesus prophesied:

[B]elieve me, a time is coming when you will worship the Father neither on this mountain nor in Jerusalem. [A] time is coming and has now come when the true worshipers will worship the Father in the Spirit and in truth, for they are the kind of worshipers the Father seeks. God is spirit, and his worshipers must worship in the Spirit and in truth. (John 4:21, 23, 24)

"[B]elieve me, a time is coming when you will worship the Father neither on this mountain nor in Jerusalem." With the New Covenant, worship of the Almighty would no longer be confined to the temple in Jerusalem. For, the Son of God ushered in the global temple of the living God through the baptism of the Holy Spirit. Simultaneously, Jesus Christ ushered in a new form of worship: by the same Holy Spirit with which we are baptized.

Jesus prophesied: "God is spirit, and his worshipers must worship in the Spirit and in truth." This prophecy is directly connected to Jesus' prophecy of the Comforter: "I will ask the Father and he will give you another Comforter, and he will never leave you. He is the Holy Spirit, the Spirit who leads into all truth" (John 14:16).

All the revelation Christ gave about the Holy Spirit to His apostles expounds upon His original prophecy: "the true worshipers will worship the Father in the Spirit and in truth."

Christ gave unique revelation to His apostles to form a unified picture of what it means to worship God in the Spirit and in truth. Look at how Paul connected the temple of God with the

Holy Spirit that dwells in us:

> Do you not know *and* understand that you
> [the church] are the temple of God, and that
> the Spirit of God dwells [permanently] in
> you [collectively and individually]? (1 Cor.
> 6:16)

Christ's revelation on the Holy Spirit is given
to open our eyes to true worship.

Embrace it. Revel in it. See it fulfilled in your
life.

Now, consider the revelation Jesus gave on
the very day He ascended into Heaven: "[F]or
John truly baptized with water, but you shall be
baptized with the Holy Spirit not many days
from now" (Acts 1:5). And on that day, Jesus also
prophesied: "These signs will accompany those
who believe... they will speak in new tongues"
(Mark 16:17).

How important are prophecies given by the
Son of God on the day of His Ascension?

The prophecy of being baptized in the Holy
Spirit signaled how we would worship God in the
Spirit. The prophecy of "new tongues" signaled a
new form of worship: by the language (tongue)
of the Holy Spirit.

In the revelation Christ gave to Paul, Christ
described how speaking in new tongues is
worship:

> For one who speaks in an [unknown] tongue
> speaks not to men but to God, for no one

understands or catches his meaning, because in the [Holy] Spirit he utters secret truths and hidden things [not obvious to the understanding]. (1 Cor. 14:2)

Speaking in new tongues is direct, spiritual communication with God, worshipping God by speaking "secret truths" and "hidden things." These secret truths and hidden things are spoken in the language of the Holy Spirit—which is perfect. Thus, speaking in new tongues is perfect worship of the Almighty in the temple of the living God!

In addition, not only is speaking in new tongues a new form of worship, it is a supernatural sign. God's Son gave us the assurance that although He was leaving Earth, He would still be present with us by way of the Holy Spirit and the supernatural sign of its indwelling presence: "speaking in new tongues."

A Divine Sign

What separates Jesus Christ from every other prophet is that He rose from the dead and ascended into Heaven. Although some people render this divine revelation to be a story, those who embrace the Son of God know it to be true. Heaven has given Earth a supernatural sign that Jesus is Earth's Messiah.

Through the indwelling Holy Spirit, a son of God is empowered to bring forth a divine sign:

speaking in tongues (divinely inspired languages). This language is divine because it is of the Holy Spirit. These divine languages are known by God, but not by the one speaking. Thus, speaking in a divine language is a supernatural sign from God.

This sign of tongues is a sign of Christ's Resurrection from the dead. For the only way to speak forth a divine language is through the Holy Spirit, and the only way to be filled with the Holy Spirit is if Jesus Christ baptized you with it. And the only way He could baptize you with it is if He was resurrected and ascended to the right hand of God.

The Grandeur and Surpassing Greatness of the Power

We, as God's creation, are earthen vessels. Our treasure in earthen vessels is "the knowledge of the glory and majesty of God [clearly revealed] in the face of Christ" (2 Cor. 4:6). In addition, our treasure is the "grandeur and surpassing greatness of the power [shown to be] from God" (2 Cor. 4:7).

In the knowledge of glory and majesty of God is found a mystery—a supernatural sign— which reveals the grandeur and surpassing greatness of power shown to be from God. This supernatural sign was hidden within the mystery; it is a treasure of knowledge once hidden in Christ which He did not reveal until the very day of His Ascension into Heaven.

This supernatural sign would testify to the Good News of the gospel of grace. In other words, God would testify to the world that His salvation through Christ would be backed up by visible, supernatural power. That is precisely what the New Testament reveals:

> This salvation, which was first announced by the Lord, was confirmed to us by those who heard him. God also testified to it by signs, wonders and various miracles, and by gifts of the Holy Spirit distributed according to his will. (Heb. 2:3, 4)

In the first century A.D., God testified to His salvation—and He continues to testify in the twenty-first century. Any thought to the contrary has no scriptural basis.

Regarding the gifts of the Holy Spirit, Paul said all gifts will remain within the kingdom until Christ is revealed and the kingdom is raptured. Paul's prophecy is unmistakable:

> For in him [Christ] you have been enriched in every way—with all kinds of speech and with all knowledge—God thus confirming our testimony about Christ among you. Therefore you do not lack any spiritual gift as you eagerly wait for our Lord Jesus Christ to be revealed. (1 Cor. 1:5–7)

Paul handed us Christ's revelation. If Paul said, "you do not lack any spiritual gift as you eagerly wait for our Lord Jesus Christ to be revealed" then logically, until our Lord Jesus Christ is revealed, His kingdom cannot lack any spiritual gift. Thereby, God continues to demonstrate the grandeur and surpassing greatness of His power by all gifts of the Holy Spirit (1 Cor. 12:7–11), including the gift of speaking in tongues.

In the first century A.D., the apostles were revolutionary. Never in recorded history had man spoken forth a language inspired by the Holy Spirit born within. In the twenty-first century, it is still revolutionary to speak forth a language inspired by the Holy Spirit.

This is the supreme authority of Scripture: Our King gave this divine sign to His kingdom in the first century, and it remains just as valid in the twenty-first century. Everything the Son of God heralded about the Good News is still the Good News. To be "born again" is Good News. To store up "treasures in Heaven" is Good News. To "speak in new tongues" is Good News. *It's all good news.*

Let me share with you a story about a seasoned minister, a dear friend of mine, Dr. Arthur Rouner. He was searching for greater understanding of this sign of new tongues.

After serving for many years as a Congregational minister, Dr. Rouner attended a renewal at a Catholic seminary connected with St. John's University. At that renewal, he was eager to hear more about the prophecy of speaking in tongues.

While at lunch with fellow ministers, he shared his lack of clarity on the matter. He even wondered if he was a good candidate for such a gift. In the same breath, he heard back the following wisdom, "any and every Christian may and can receive the baptism and have the gift of tongues—and, of course, other gifts as well."[20]

Soon thereafter, a Lutheran minister walked with Dr. Rouner onto the lawn which was set below the great abbey church. The Lutheran minister explained the language of the Spirit was "already there, down inside."[21] He then prayed over Arthur.

Following this, Arthur stated: "I mumbled in response a few syllables which seemed strange and stumbling and totally inadequate to me."[22]

The Lutheran minister responded, "That's right. That's a start. All you have to do now is practice your new language, go in peace, and be glad!"[23] Dr. Rouner described speaking in a divine language as a "freeing and healing personal experience."[24] I second that.

Dr. Rouner broke through the walls of his own religious tradition and fulfilled Christ's prophecy. He then moved forward with his ministry, praying over many in his congregation who would also speak in divine languages.

Like Dr. Rouner, I was also searching. In 1980, Christ baptized me with His Holy Spirit, and soon thereafter I spoke forth the sign of tongues. I too witnessed my divine language begin with just a few syllables. I learned that the mechanics of speech are the same—whether you are speaking your native language or speaking your divine language, you are in control, and you breathe and speak what is already within you.

How do you think I felt after I fulfilled a prophecy spoken by the Son of God? Peacefulness and overwhelming joy! Without question, the grandeur and surpassing greatness of this power was shown to be from God. He demonstrated it by a divine sign: the gift of speaking in tongues.

Thankfully, there is no need to wonder about God testifying in your life through the gift of tongues. Christ made known the will of the Holy Spirit. By revelation, Paul said: "I would like every one of you to speak in tongues" (1 Cor. 14:5). That's the truth. Not a single Scripture— stated before or after—contradicts Paul's clear statement.

"I would like every one of you to speak in tongues" means "I would like every one of you to speak in tongues."

Why should anyone be surprised at the will of the Holy Spirit? Speaking in new tongues is direct, spiritual communication with God. Why would God deny anyone in His kingdom this glorious form of worship? He wouldn't.

The Gift of Speaking in Tongues

It was from Heaven, that Christ gave Paul

the abundance of the revelation on speaking in tongues. Paul said: "Now about the spiritual *gifts* [the special endowments given by the Holy Spirit], brothers and sisters, I do not want you to be uninformed" (1 Cor. 12:1). "[T]o each one the manifestation of the Spirit is given for the common good" (1 Cor. 12:7). This includes "speaking in different kinds of tongues" (1 Cor. 12:10). In other words, the Spirit is manifested, or demonstrated, by speaking in the Spirit. It is also demonstrated by praying and singing in the Spirit.

> I [Paul] will pray with my spirit [by the Holy Spirit that is within me], but I will also pray [intelligently] with my mind and understanding; I will sing with my spirit [by the Holy Spirit that is within me], but I will sing [intelligently] with my mind and understanding also. (1 Cor. 14:15)

Singing is a form of worship: "come before his presence with singing" (Ps. 100:2). And singing in the language of the Spirit is perfect worship.

Prayer is a form of worship: "Paul and Silas were praying and singing hymns to God" (Acts 16:25). And praying in the language of the Spirit is perfect worship.

Speaking unto God is a form of worship: "I cried out to him with my mouth; his praise was on my tongue" (Ps. 66:17). And speaking by the language of the Spirit is perfect worship.

Paul worshipped God by singing, praying, and speaking by the language of his own mind, and by singing, praying, and speaking by the language of the Holy Spirit. And Paul said: "Pattern yourselves after me [follow my example], as I imitate *and* follow Christ (the Messiah)" (1 Cor. 11:1). Paul's revelation about worshipping the Almighty in the language of the Spirit is ours to embrace.

Paul's revelation about the gift of tongues is in complete harmony with all the revelation Christ gave in the Holy Land, and with the Old Testament, and with the testimony in the Acts of the Apostles.

Acts of the Apostles

The book in the Bible known as the Acts of the Apostles documents the apostles' acts in the first century A.D. It is not just a history book. It is our standard for right application of sound doctrine in the twenty-first century. The letters written by Paul and the prophecies of Christ confirm this.

In the Acts of the Apostles, the Son of God issued a prophecy to His disciples on the day of His Ascension: "[Y]ou shall receive power when the Holy Spirit has come upon you" (Acts 1:8).

When this prophecy came to pass (ten days after the Ascension) the history of mankind witnessed dramatic divine intervention. Man's future was forever altered. Peter and the other eleven apostles were the first among Christ's followers to "receive power."

The twelve apostles spoke forth this divine sign of divine languages on the holy day of Pentecost. (Pentecost was ten days after Christ's ascension and fifty days after the Resurrection.) On that day, man's great high priest—Jesus Christ—baptized His apostles with the Holy Spirit.

Before this prophecy came to pass, the risen Messiah prepared His apostles for Pentecost. The Lord told them:

> Do not leave Jerusalem, but wait for the gift my Father promised, which you have heard me speak about. For John baptized with water, but in a few days you will be baptized with the Holy Spirit. You will receive power when the Holy Spirit comes on you; and you will be my witnesses in Jerusalem, and in all Judea and Samaria, and to the ends of the earth. (Acts 1:4, 5, 8)

> "I am going to send you what my Father has promised; but stay in the city until you have been clothed with power from on high." When he had led them out to the vicinity of Bethany, he lifted up his hands and blessed them. While he was blessing them, he left them and was taken up into heaven. Then they worshiped him and returned to Jerusalem with great joy. And they stayed continually at the temple, praising God.

(Luke 24:49–53)

As Christ lifted off to the clouds, the apostles stood staring into Heaven with the assurance that their Lord would fulfill His promise. Then, the apostles stayed "continually at the temple" because that's where man's great high priest would clothe the Twelve with "power from on high."

After Christ ascended, Peter prepared for the fulfillment of Christ's prophecy. This included selecting a new apostle—Matthias—to replace Judas Iscariot. Peter declared to a multitude of faithful followers (about 120 people), that Matthias would become a witness of the Resurrection with him and the other apostles. On the eve of Pentecost, Peter addressed the followers of Jesus:

"It is necessary to choose one of the men who have been with us the whole time the Lord Jesus went in and out among us, beginning from John's baptism to the time when Jesus was taken up from us. For one of these must become a witness with us of his resurrection." Then they cast lots, and the lot fell to Matthias; so he was added to the eleven apostles. (Acts 1:21, 22, 26)

When the day of Pentecost came, they were all together in one place. Suddenly a sound like the blowing of a violent wind came from heaven and filled the whole house where they were sitting. They saw what seemed to be tongues of fire that separated and came to rest on each of them. All of them were filled with the Holy Spirit and began to speak in other tongues as the Spirit enabled them. (Acts 2:1–4)

The spiritual shock of all ages burst upon the house of prayer during an hour of prayer. As powerful winds rushed throughout the corridors, flaming tongues of fire burned above the twelve men. With the visual sign of tongues given, the twelve apostles spoke forth new tongues, becoming witnesses of the Resurrection by the sign of the Resurrection.

As caravans of devout followers of Moses traveled from many countries, making their pilgrimage to the temple in Jerusalem, they had no idea what awaited them on Pentecost. As thousands of people gathered in quiet adoration to pray at the temple, heavenly signs shattered the silence. At nine o'clock in the morning, God sent an unmistakable exclamation mark shooting through the hearts of all the worshipers present. The prophecies of the Old Testament regarding the first coming of Christ and His New Covenant had been fulfilled completely.

Where else would God Almighty usher in *His New Covenant worship* but at *His house of worship*, the temple: the "house of prayer" (Matt. 21:13)?!

Where did the apostles stay continually after Jesus ascended off the planet, but at the "temple" (Luke 24:53)?!

Where else would the apostles be on the holy day of Pentecost (the Feast of Weeks), but at the temple—praying during an hour of prayer?!

Where else could thousands of followers of the Old Covenant witness God's fulfillment of prophecy but at the temple?!

By way of the apostles, God spoke to thousands of His followers at His house of prayer. Inspired by the Holy Spirit within, the men from Galilee spoke multiple foreign languages and people from many nations heard God speak. Thousands of people heard the wonderful works of God spoken in their ears in their native languages.

Pentecost was the unmistakable line of demarcation, separating the Law from faith. No longer would righteousness be earned, rather, it would be granted by faith. This outpouring of the Spirit established the New Covenant with mankind. Christ's kingdom would now worship in the living temple of the living God, as this temple would be built not by stones but by the baptism of Holy Spirit—and it would be made known to the world by divine signs.

The indwelling Spirit of Christ enabled the Twelve to speak in new languages, but it was the apostles themselves who actually spoke the sign of tongues into being. The Holy Spirit did not control them. The apostles were in control of their own act of speaking. As explained by Paul, "the spirits of the prophets are subject to the prophets" (1 Cor. 14:32). After Christ filled the

Twelve with His Spirit, the apostles spoke the sign into evidence.

This mystifying display of supernatural energy in the temple caused the onlookers to be struck with disbelief:

> Now there were staying in Jerusalem God-fearing Jews from every nation under heaven. When they heard this sound, a crowd came together in bewilderment, because each one heard them speaking in his own language. Utterly amazed, they asked: "Are not all these men who are speaking Galileans? Then how is it that each of us hears them in his own native language?" (Acts 2:5–8)

> "[W]e hear them declaring the wonders of God in our own tongues!" Amazed and perplexed, they asked one another, "What does this mean?" Some, however, made fun of them and said, "They have had too much wine." Then Peter stood up with the Eleven, raised his voice, and addressed the crowd: "Fellow Jews and all of you who live in Jerusalem, let me explain this to you; listen carefully to what I say. These men are not drunk, as you suppose. It's only nine in the morning! No, this is what was spoken by the prophet Joel:

> 'In the last days, God says, I will pour out my Spirit on all people. Even on my servants,

both men and women, I will pour out my Spirit in those days, and they will prophesy. I will show wonders in the heavens above and signs on the earth below, blood and fire and billows of smoke. The sun will be turned to darkness and the moon to blood before the coming of the great and glorious day of the Lord. And everyone who calls on the name of the Lord will be saved.'" (Acts 2:11–21)

In order to establish the significance of what the crowd witnessed, Peter quoted the prophet Joel, one of the Old Testament prophets. Peter told the crowd that they had heard divine prophecy fulfilled in their ears.

Hundreds of years before Christ, Joel foretold of the day God would pour out his Spirit upon flesh and blood. Joel recorded the very words spoken by the Almighty: "I will pour out my Spirit on all people. Even on my servants, both men and women, I will pour out my Spirit in those days" (Joel 2:28, 29). On Pentecost this prophecy came to pass.

Not only did Peter declare the fulfillment of Joel's prophecy (with the Spirit being poured out), Peter continued to quote Joel to complete what God will accomplish: "And everyone who calls on the name of the Lord will be saved."

In other words, Peter quoted a unique section of Joel. He told the crowd at the temple that God had given birth to a new kingdom (those filled with His Spirit), and how those in the kingdom would prophesy, and how all in the kingdom (those who call on the name of the Lord) would ultimately be saved (raptured) on the day of the Lord! It was the mystery revealed.

By way of Peter, the Lord God heralded the mystery of the church to His faithful followers who gathered at the temple from over the known world.

By way of the Twelve, the Lord God spoke in various tongues to all of those who sought Him—testifying that Jesus was the Christ.

This holy day of Pentecost represented fulfillment of not only Joel's prophecy, but that of Isaiah's as well: "With foreign lips and strange tongues God will speak to this people, to whom he said, 'This is the resting place, let the weary rest'; and, 'This is the place of repose'—but they would not listen" (Isa. 28:11, 12). This is exactly what Paul quoted in his letter:

> In the Law it is written: "With other tongues and through the lips of foreigners I will speak to this people, but even then they will not listen to me, says the Lord." Tongues, then, are a sign, not for believers but for unbelievers. (1 Cor. 14:21, 22)

God fulfilled His promise. He said that He would bring rest and repose (refreshing) to His people, and speak to His people with "foreign lips" and "strange tongues." On Pentecost, this prophecy of new languages was fulfilled. Yet for all of this, Isaiah foretold that there would be followers of Moses who would not embrace even a supernatural sign from God. On Pentecost, some devout followers of the Old Covenant even accused Peter of being drunk when he spoke in tongues.

Peter shrugged off the accusations and took center stage as he stood up to address the crowd. All eyes were riveted on Peter as he began to teach about Jesus Christ and eternal life. Without hesitation, he set in order the things pertaining to this Jesus of Nazareth and the New Covenant that He had established on Earth. The result of this great oration was the acceptance of the covenant by thousands of people on that one day.

Interestingly, just fifty days earlier, this same Peter had been hiding behind locked doors, "for fear of the Jewish leaders" (John 20:19). Peter had even denied knowing the Lord; he had nothing to say publicly concerning Him. With the Crucifixion of Jesus, Peter and the others had been overcome with grief and loss. But now, infused with spiritual power from on high, Peter changed from a man controlled by fear to a man of great confidence and faith. Only one thing could have changed him—Pentecost— and Peter began teaching boldly in the name of Christ.

Peter had a new set of eyes with which to view life. The apostle looked quite differently on those whom he once feared when he gave the crowd prophetic knowledge:

Men of Israel, listen to this: Jesus of Nazareth was a man accredited by God to you by miracles, wonders and signs, which God did among you through him, as you yourselves know. This man was handed over to you by God's set purpose and foreknowledge; and you, with the help of wicked men, put him to death by nailing him to the cross. But God raised him from the dead, freeing him from the agony of death, because it was impossible for death to keep its hold on him. God has raised this Jesus to life, and we are all witnesses of the fact. Exalted to the right hand of God, he has received from the Father the promised Holy Spirit and has poured out what you now see and hear. (Acts 2:22–24, 32, 33)

Therefore, let all Israel be assured of this: God has made this Jesus, whom you crucified, both Lord and Christ. When the people heard this, they were cut to the heart and said to Peter and the other apostles, "Brothers, what shall we do?" Peter replied, "Repent and be baptized, every one of you, in the name of Jesus Christ for the forgiveness of your sins. And you will receive the gift of the Holy Spirit. The promise is for you and your children and for all who are far off—for all whom the Lord our God will call." With many other words he warned them; and he pleaded with them: "Save yourselves from this corrupt generation." Those who accepted his message were baptized, and about three thousand were added to their number that day. (Acts 2:36–41)

"Brothers, what shall we do?"

"Repent and be baptized, every one of you, in the name of Jesus Christ for the forgiveness of your sins. And you will receive the gift of the Holy Spirit."

This question and Peter's response are just as alive and real today as they were some two thousand years ago. The promises of God are unchanging.

On the first day of the "church," about three thousand people in the temple area believed Peter and received the Holy Spirit. Imagine what could have been going through the mind of Peter. Ten days earlier, he had watched Christ ascend off the planet. Now Jerusalem was filled with the presence of Heaven, and it would soon overflow into every bloodline.

Divine intervention assured that the apostles received the inspiration they needed to carry forth what Christ had initiated on Pentecost. As documented in the Acts of the Apostles, Peter received revelation from Christ in the form of a vision, directing him to take the gospel of grace to the Romans. Upon his arrival at the home of a Roman soldier, Peter expounded upon the will of God:

"I now realize how true it is that God does not show favoritism but accepts men from every nation who fear him and do what is right. You know the message God sent to the people of Israel, telling the good news of peace through Jesus Christ, who is Lord of all. You know what has happened throughout Judea, beginning in Galilee after the baptism that John preached—how God anointed Jesus of Nazareth with the Holy Spirit and power, and how he went around doing good and healing all who were under the power of the devil, because God was with him. We are witnesses of everything he did in the country of the Jews and in Jerusalem. They killed him by hanging him on a tree, but God raised him from the dead on the third day and caused him to be seen. He was not seen by all the people, but by witnesses whom God had already chosen—by us who ate and drank with him after he rose from the dead. He commanded us to preach to the people and to testify that he is the one whom God appointed as judge of the living and the dead. All the prophets testify about him that everyone who believes in him receives forgiveness of sins through his name." While Peter was still speaking these words, the Holy Spirit came on all who heard the message. The circumcised believers who had come with Peter were astonished that the gift of the Holy Spirit had been poured out even on the Gentiles. For they heard them speaking in tongues and praising God. (Acts 10:34–46)

After Peter taught the words of Christ, the Romans manifested the sign of tongues. No one was denied entrance into the kingdom of God, and no one was denied its sign. This is the New Covenant that Christ gave to every nation, to every bloodline.

As Peter demonstrated the truth of Christ's gospel, so did Paul. When Paul visited the city of Ephesus, he taught twelve disciples about Christ's baptism, and they spoke forth the gift of tongues:

> Paul took the road through the interior and arrived at Ephesus. There he found some disciples and asked them, "Did you receive the Holy Spirit when you believed?"
>
> They answered, "No, we have not even heard that there is a Holy Spirit."
> So Paul asked, "Then what baptism did you receive?"
>
> "John's baptism," they replied.
>
> Paul said, "John's baptism was a baptism of repentance. He told the people to believe in the one coming after him, that is, in Jesus."
>
> On hearing this, they were baptized into the name of the Lord Jesus. When Paul placed his hands on them, the Holy Spirit came on them, and they spoke in tongues and

prophesied. (Acts 19:1–6)

Paul asked a question: "Did you receive the Holy Spirit when you believed?" This question is just as valid today as it was in the first century A.D.

What does "receive the Holy Spirit" mean? Certainly it means to be baptized with Holy Spirit. Yet, there was more to the story with these believers in Ephesus. It has to do with God testifying to salvation. To "receive" the Holy Spirit literally means "to take what is given pointing to an objective reception."[25] In other words, receiving the Holy Spirit speaks of manifesting the Holy Spirit. That is precisely what speaking in tongues is: a "manifestation of the Spirit" (1 Cor. 12:7).

Paul explained to these disciples exactly what John the Baptist explained: Water baptism would be superseded by the spiritual baptism of Christ, and God testified to it by the sign of tongues. John said:

> I [John] baptize you with water for repentance. But after me will come one who is more powerful than I, whose sandals I am not fit to carry. He will baptize you with the Holy Spirit and with fire. (Matt. 3:11)

The Son of God baptized the apostles with the Holy Spirit and they spoke in tongues. Christ baptized Cornelius and his company with Holy Spirit and they spoke in tongues. Christ baptized the Ephesians with Holy Spirit and they spoke in tongues. God testified to their salvation by the power that is unmistakably His—and thank God, His will hasn't changed.

The Will of God

Before concluding this chapter, it is vitally important to first address the will of God for the assembly of believers.

After revealing the will of God (through the Holy Spirit) for individual believers, Paul revealed the will of God for the assembly of believers. Paul said:

> I would like every one of you to speak in tongues, but I would rather have you prophesy. The one who prophesies is greater than the one who speaks in tongues, unless someone interprets, so that the church may be edified. (1 Cor. 14:5)

This is the will of God for individuals: "I would like every one of you to speak in tongues."

This is the will of God for the assembly of believers: "I would rather have you prophesy. The one who prophesies is greater than the one who speaks in tongues, unless someone interprets, so that the church may be edified."

The will of God for the assembly and for individuals is revealed: They are different and each truth stands on its own merit. The goal is the same: edification (which means to strengthen). The individual is strengthened by speaking in tongues, and the assembly is strengthened by prophesy and/or speaking in tongues with interpretation.

In addition to the will of God for spiritual gifts, there is the will of God for gift ministries in the church for the assembly of believers. Importantly, there is the gift ministry of tongues designed to benefit the assembly (the body of Christ). Regarding gift ministries and the will of God, Paul said:

> Now you are the body of Christ, and each one of you is a part of it. And God has placed in the church first of all apostles, second prophets, third teachers, then miracles, then gifts of healing, of helping, of guidance, and of different kinds of tongues. Are all apostles? Are all prophets? Are all teachers? Do all work miracles? Do all have gifts of healing? Do all speak in tongues? Do all interpret? Now eagerly desire the greater gifts. (1 Cor. 12:27–31)

This section of Scripture is about gift ministries which are placed by God in the church. These are unique ministries given by God where they are needed. "Do all speak with tongues?" refers to the gift ministry of tongues in the church. "Do all speak with tongues?" The answer is no; not every ministry is a gift ministry of tongues.

Conversely, "I would like every one of you to speak in tongues" (1 Cor. 14:5) refers to the gift of speaking in tongues which is distributed by the Holy Spirit, available to every individual believer.

In this light, "I would like every one of you to speak in tongues" and "Do all speak in tongues?" do not contradict one another. Each refers to an entirely different function and purpose in the kingdom.

The First Century and the Twenty-first Century

In the first century, Paul gave us what we needed to know about the will of God and the gifts. Yet, before the end of his life, Paul suffered the loss of loyalty from those he taught, and many in the kingdom turned away from him. Paul wrote: "You know that everyone in the province of Asia has deserted me" (2 Tim. 1:15).

Abandoning Paul meant abandoning Paul's revelation. The implications are staggering.

Dr. Rouner and I both grew up with a Christian tradition that did not promote the gift of tongues. For each of us, fulfilling prophecy began with listening to the Scriptures, not religious tradition.

The Scriptures reveal the truth: "God is spirit, and his worshipers must worship in the Spirit and in truth" (John 4:24). And God testifies to salvation "by signs, wonders and various miracles, and by gifts of the Holy Spirit distributed according to his will" (Heb. 2:4).

Speaking in new tongues is exactly what Christ said it is: a sign. (The sign of tongues is not a requirement for salvation, but rather testifies to that salvation.) The supernatural sign of tongues is the irrefutable statement from God that the one speaking has entered the eternal kingdom of Christ and shall live to see the new Earth. And yes, that changes you!

If you would like to speak forth this divine sign of tongues, you are at the same place I once was, as well as Dr. Rouner. Follow Paul's inspiration: Follow the love of God and "earnestly desire and cultivate the spiritual endowments (gifts)" (1 Cor. 14:1).

God bless the truth: The divine sign of tongues will continue until Christ the King is seen "face to face" (1 Cor. 13:12). It is then we will "know fully" (1 Cor. 13:12). It is then we will no longer need a sign of salvation—because He will bring us to His throne!

> So I [Jesus] say to you: Ask and it will be given to you; seek and you will find; knock and the door will be opened to you. For everyone who asks receives; the one who seeks finds; and to the one who knocks, the door will be opened. Which of you fathers, if your son asks for a fish, will give him a snake instead? Or if he asks for an egg, will give him a scorpion? If you then, though you are

evil, know how to give good gifts to your children, how much more will your Father in heaven give the Holy Spirit to those who ask him! (Luke 11:9–13)

A Prayer

May God be gracious to us and bless us and make his face shine on us—so that your ways may be known on earth, your salvation among all nations. (Ps. 67:1, 2)

Trust in the Lord with all your heart, And lean not on your own understanding; In all your ways acknowledge Him, And He shall direct your paths. (Prov. 3:5, 6)

Epilogue

The Chronology of Prophecy

> Blessed is he who reads and those who hear the words of this prophecy, and keep those things which are written in it; for the time is near.
>
> —The Apostle John (Rev. 1:3)

At the end of the first century, the Son of God descended from Heaven and appeared in His glorified form to John. It was during this appearance that Christ revealed the chronological sequence of end-time events, providing a virtual motion picture of the drama that shall unfold on Earth and what waits in the hereafter. With this divine revelation, John would write the last book of the Bible: Revelation.

Significantly, Revelation is the only book in the Bible that marks end-time prophecies with a numbered sequence. Why else would Christ number the prophecies but to show us the chronological order of end-time events?

Christ's final revelation to John marks the last book of the Bible, but it is the first place we look to understand how all the pieces of the end-time puzzle given by both the prophets and apostles fit together. In essence, Christ's final revelation to us is the key that unlocks the entire Bible regarding Heaven's intervention into earthly affairs during the end times. Every end-time prophecy drops right into the numbered chronology of Revelation, which begins with the first seal.

Revelation

In the opening chapter of Revelation, John prophesied of what shall come to pass for those in the King's kingdom:

> John, To the seven churches in the province of Asia: Grace and peace to you from him who is, and who was, and who is to come, and from the seven spirits before his throne, and from Jesus Christ, who is the faithful witness, the firstborn from the dead, and the ruler of the kings of the earth. To him who loves us and has freed us from our sins by his blood, and has made us to be a kingdom and priests to serve his God and Father—to him be glory and power for ever and ever! Amen. "Look, he is coming with the clouds," and "every eye will see him, even those who pierced him"; and all peoples on earth "will mourn because of him." So shall it be! Amen. (Rev. 1:4–7)

John wrote to all those cleansed by the blood of Christ who entered the King's kingdom. He wrote to the same audience as Peter: those "who have been chosen according to the foreknowledge of God the Father, through the sanctifying work of the Spirit, to be obedient to Jesus Christ and sprinkled with his blood" (1 Peter 1:2). And John wrote to the same audience as Paul: "to those sanctified in Christ Jesus and called to be his holy people, together with all those everywhere who call on the name of our Lord Jesus Christ—their Lord and ours" (1 Cor. 1:2).

John, Peter, and Paul received revelation from Christ and all three apostles were in complete agreement. Each apostle was given unique revelation that fit together, perfectly.

John prophesied of Christ's appearing in the clouds (Rev. 1:7) just as Paul did (1 Thess. 4:13–17), but each provided different details. John prophesied of the sun turning black and the moon turning blood red (Rev. 6:12) just as Peter did (Acts 2:20), but each provided different details.

Like Paul, John acknowledged the source of his revelation: Christ. John recorded the appearance of the glorified Christ, describing Him as human-like in organization but entirely spiritual in nature. Not only did John see his Lord but he also witnessed firsthand the spiritual body that awaits those who shall live eternally.

On the Lord's Day I [John] was in the Spirit, and I heard behind me a loud voice like a trumpet, which said: "Write on a scroll what you see and send it to the seven churches: to Ephesus, Smyrna, Pergamum, Thyatira, Sardis, Philadelphia and Laodicea." I turned around to see the voice that was speaking to me. And when I turned I saw someone like a son of man, dressed in a robe reaching down to his feet and with a golden sash around his chest. His head and hair were white like wool, as white as snow, and his eyes were like blazing fire. His feet were like bronze glowing in a furnace, and his voice was like the sound of rushing waters. His face was like the sun shining in all its brilliance. When I saw him, I fell at his feet as though dead. Then he placed his right hand on me and said: "Do not be afraid. I am the First and the Last. I am the Living One; I was dead, and behold I am alive for ever and ever!" (Rev. 1:10–18)

The now-glorified Christ stood before John to impart divine revelation by way of visions. Christ told John: "Write the things which you have seen, and the things which are, and the things which will take place after this" (Rev. 1:19).

This chapter focuses on "the things which will take place after this": prophecy. The presentation began after John stepped through a door in his mind to Heaven.

After this I [John] looked, and there before me was a door standing open in heaven. And the voice I had first heard speaking to me like a trumpet said, "Come up here, and I will show you what must take place after this." At once I was in the Spirit, and there before me was a throne in heaven with someone sitting on it. And the one who sat there had the appearance of jasper and carnelian [precious stones]. A rainbow, resembling an emerald, encircled the throne. Then I saw in the right hand of him who sat on the throne a scroll with writing on both sides and sealed with seven seals. (Rev. 4:1–3; 5:1)

John saw the throne of God. Imagine.

John then saw in the hand of Him a scroll "sealed with seven seals." As this scroll opened, so was John's mind opened to divine intervention. With each seal, John saw moving pictures that reached deeper and deeper into the future.

The futuristic scene began after the first four seals opened, and God released His horsemen. John saw the "Four Horsemen of the Apocalypse" loosed upon Earth to fulfill God's will.

The Four Horsemen

I [John] watched as the Lamb [Christ] opened the first of the seven seals. Then I heard one of the four living creatures say in a voice like thunder, "Come!" I looked, and there before me was a white horse! Its rider held a bow, and he was given a crown, and he rode out as a conqueror bent on conquest. When the Lamb opened the second seal, I heard the second living creature say, "Come!" Then another horse came out, a fiery red one. Its rider was given power to take peace from the earth and to make men slay each other. To him was given a large sword. When the Lamb opened the third seal, I heard the third living creature say, "Come!" I looked, and there before me was a black horse! Its rider was holding a pair of scales in his hand. When the Lamb opened the fourth seal, I heard the voice of the fourth living creature say, "Come!" I looked, and there before me was a pale horse! Its rider was named Death, and Hades [the grave] was following close behind him. They were given power over a fourth of the earth to kill by sword, famine and plague, and by the wild beasts of the earth. (Rev. 6:1–5, 7, 8)

Centuries before this prophecy, the prophet Zechariah spoke of the horsemen: "These are the four spirits of heaven, going out from standing in the presence of the Lord of the whole world" (Zech. 6:5).

The four horsemen shall prepare Earth for the most dramatic event modern man has ever witnessed: the appearance of Jesus Christ (which shall occur after the sixth seal opens). (Note: There are no visible heavenly or earthly signs that accompany the four horsemen.)

With the four horsemen upon Earth, only one seal will separate the population from the appearing of Christ: the fifth. It represents the last "invisible" mark on the heavenly clock. It is the final unseen sign.

The Fifth Seal

> When he opened the fifth seal, I saw under the altar the souls of those who had been slain for the word of God and the testimony they had maintained. They called out in a loud voice, "How long, Sovereign Lord, holy and true, until you judge the inhabitants of the earth and avenge our blood?" Then each of them was given a white robe, and they were told to wait a little longer, until the number of their fellow servants and brothers who were to be killed as they had been was completed. (Rev. 6:9–11)

The prayer of the martyred will soon be answered; God's assurance is that the martyrs need only wait "a little longer" for the judgment they seek because justice shall be delivered after the seventh seal opens.

With the martyrs' prayer in Heaven and the four horsemen fulfilling their charge on Earth, the stage is then set for the appearing of God's Son, and, unlike the first five seals, when the sixth seal is loosed, it will shock the population. The sixth seal not only marks the appearing of Christ for His kingdom, but also announces the coming wrath (judgment).

The Sixth Seal

> I [John] watched as he opened the sixth seal. There was a great earthquake. The sun turned black like sackcloth made of goat hair, the whole moon turned blood red, and the stars in the sky fell to earth, as figs drop from a fig tree when shaken by a strong wind. The heavens receded like a scroll being rolled up, and every mountain and island was removed from its place. (Rev. 6:12–14)

When darkness surrounds the planet, the moon turns blood red, stars shoot upon the horizon, and every mountain and island shift from a massive earthquake, the deceptive calm upon Earth shall end abruptly. With this colossal presentation, God shall put the nations on notice that a threshold has been reached: Divine intervention shall rescue those who pursued righteousness, and divine judgment shall be upon those who rejected it.

When the sixth seal opens, everyone on the planet will fulfill prophecy.

All on the planet are viewed by God by their belief system. And according to Him, there are three distinct groups of people on Earth: the kingdom of Christ (church of God), the twelve tribes of Israel (i.e., the Jews), and everyone else (referred to as the Gentiles). This is precisely how God refers to His creation: "the Jews, the Gentiles, [and] the church of God" (1 Cor. 10:32).

With the opening of the sixth seal, all three groups will be affected. In John's opening vision, he first sees the effects of the sixth seal upon the Gentiles.

The Gentiles

> And the kings of the earth, and the great men, and the rich men, and the chief captains, and the mighty men, and every bondman, and every free man, hid themselves in the dens and in the rocks of the mountains; and said to the mountains and rocks, Fall on us, and hide us from the face of him that sitteth on the throne, and from the wrath of the Lamb: for the great day of his wrath is come; and who shall be able to stand? (Rev. 6:15–17)

The Gentiles, who rejected "the way, the truth, and the life," will cry out, "hide us from the face of him that sitteth on the throne, and from the wrath of the Lamb."

John foresaw that the world would be locked in a stare to the heavens beholding the glorified Christ: "He is coming with the clouds, and every eye will see him" (Rev. 1:7). The response from the Gentiles is to hide from God and His Christ, whom they rejected, "for the great day of his wrath is come."

This "great day" of wrath is not a 24-hour day, but rather is the time of the Lord's intervention into earthly affairs to judge the world. It is the day of the Lord.[26] It will extend for years (as presented in Revelation's chronology).

The word "day" can mean "a period or point of time."[27] In this case, that is exactly what it means: The "day" of His wrath is the "day" of His intervention, which is a span of time that will take years to fulfill.

John's prophecy of this coming "day" reflects what was already prophesied in the Old Testament. Isaiah prophesied:

> Enter into the rock, and hide in the dust, From the terror of the Lord And the glory of His majesty. The lofty looks of man shall be humbled, The haughtiness of men shall be bowed down, And the Lord alone shall be exalted in that day. For the day of the Lord

of hosts Shall come upon everything proud and lofty, Upon everything lifted up—And it shall be brought low. They shall go into the holes of the rocks, And into the caves of the earth, From the terror of the Lord And the glory of His majesty, When He arises to shake the earth mightily. (Isa. 2:10–12, 19)

Isaiah's prophecy foretold of the day of the Lord; it is then that God will rise "to shake the Earth mightily." John's prophecy revealed exactly when this day of the Lord's judgment will be announced: when the sixth seal opens. When the sixth seal opens, nothing will be the same on Earth, and nothing will be the same in Heaven.

The Twelve Tribes of Israel

Just as the Israelites were spared from death in Egypt during the time of Pharaoh, so shall 144,000 of the twelve tribes be spared from judgment during the time of wrath. For, after the sixth seal opens, 144,000 from the tribes of Israel will be sealed by the angels: "I [John] heard the number of those who were sealed: 144,000 from all the tribes of Israel" (Rev. 7:4). This revelation was never before revealed, prior to John's prophecy.

Christ's Kingdom

There is more revelation about the day of the Lord that was never before revealed (in the Old Testament). Christ revealed to John the mystery: Hidden at the onset of the day of the Lord was the Rapture of the King's kingdom. In a vision, John saw a picture of future glory, when the kingdom will be harvested from the Earth to Heaven.

After this I looked and a vast host appeared which no one could count, [gathered out] of every nation, from all tribes and peoples and languages. These stood before the throne and before the Lamb; they were attired in white robes, with palm branches in their hands. In loud voice they cried, saying, [Our] salvation is due to our God, Who is seated on the throne, and to the Lamb [to Them we owe our deliverance]! And all the angels were standing round the throne and round the elders [of the heavenly Sanhedrin] and the four living creatures, and they fell prostrate before the throne and worshiped God. Amen! (So be it!) they cried. Blessing and glory and majesty and splendor and wisdom and thanks and honor and power and might [be ascribed] to our God to the ages and ages (forever and ever, throughout the eternities of the eternities)! Amen! (So be it!) Then, addressing me, one of the elders [of the heavenly Sanhedrin] said, Who are these [people] clothed in the long white robes? And from where have they come? I replied, Sir, you know. And he said to me, These are they who have come out of the great tribulation (persecution), and have washed their robes and made them white in the blood of the Lamb. For this reason they are [now] before the [very] throne of God and serve Him day and night in His sanctuary (temple); and He Who is sitting upon the throne will protect and spread His tabernacle over and shelter them with His presence. They shall hunger no more, neither thirst any more; neither shall the sun smite them, nor any scorching heat. For the Lamb Who is in the midst of the throne will be their Shepherd, and He will guide them to the springs of the waters of life; and God will wipe away every tear from their eyes. (Rev. 7:9–17)

This prophecy of Christ's kingdom gathered in Heaven is an expansion of prophecies already delivered by Peter and Paul.

Peter was the first apostle to herald this prophecy of future salvation on the day of the Lord, revealing the same celestial signs as John: the signs of the sun and moon.

On the first day of the church, Pentecost, Peter said:

In the last days, God says, I will pour out my

Spirit on all people. Your sons and daughters will prophesy, your young men will see visions, your old men will dream dreams. Even on my servants, both men and women, I will pour out my Spirit in those days, and they will prophesy. I will show wonders in the heavens above and signs on the earth below, blood and fire and billows of smoke. The sun will be turned to darkness and the moon to blood before the coming of the great and glorious day of the Lord. And everyone who calls on the name of the Lord will be saved. (Acts 2:17–21)

Peter quoted Joel because it was the fulfillment of Joel's prophecy. The Spirit was poured out, and it marked the first day of the church. Peter finished his quote by quoting the ultimate fulfillment of Joel's prophecy: Everyone who calls on the name of the Lord will be saved. In other words, those who are filled with the Holy Spirit are those who call on the name of the Lord, and the ultimate fulfillment of Peter's prophecy is that they will be saved on the great and glorious day of the Lord.

By quoting this section of Joel's prophecy, Peter revealed the mystery of the church hidden in the Old Testament. It was not understood until Peter's prophecy on Pentecost that God had hidden the future salvation of the church within the day of the Lord.

All prophecies about the future salvation of the church are founded on Peter's prophecy; and thus, Peter's prophecy is the key that unlocks Revelation. For Peter's prophecy identifies the exact point in time in Revelation's chronology when all who call upon the name of the Lord will be saved: when the sun turns black and the moon turns blood red.

(Incredibly, Peter's prophecy and John's prophecy are not part of the theological discussion contained in the three theories of the Rapture: "pre-tribulation," "mid-tribulation," and "post-tribulation." All three theories fail to factor in Peter's prophecy and John's prophecy into their formulas. Thus, not one of the theories recognizes the sixth seal as the time of the Rapture.)

Everything stated about the sixth seal is literal: the celestial signs and a great earthquake, the response on Earth to flee in fear, the sealing of the 144,000, and Christ's kingdom in Heaven. No symbolism is implied or stated.

Importantly, John's prophecy is in complete agreement with Paul's prophecy of the Rapture. Paul, in his prophecy about the coming day of the Lord, connected the Rapture with being saved from the wrath to come. Paul prophesied:

> For the Lord himself will come down from heaven, with a loud command, with the voice of the archangel and with the trumpet call of God, and the dead in Christ will rise first. After that, we who are still alive and are left will be caught up together with them in the clouds to meet the Lord in the air. And

so we will be with the Lord forever. Therefore encourage one another with these words. Now, brothers and sisters, about times and dates we do not need to write to you, for you know very well that the day of the Lord will come like a thief in the night. While people are saying, "Peace and safety," destruction will come on them suddenly, as labor pains on a pregnant woman, and they will not escape. But you, brothers and sisters, are not in darkness so that this day should surprise you like a thief. You are all children of the light and children of the day. We do not belong to the night or to the darkness. For God did not appoint us to suffer wrath but to receive salvation through our Lord Jesus Christ. (1 Thess. 4:16–18; 5:1–5, 9)

Arriving like "a thief in the night," the day of the Lord will come upon the world with a sudden surprise. Paul prophesied about "times and dates," not the lack of signs. The signs of the sixth seal will come upon the world without notice, and will shock the population, but the King's kingdom won't be surprised. The children of light await their Lord.

It is critical to note this: Paul's prophecy began with the Rapture and concluded with being saved from wrath. His prophecy presents a unified picture: The "effect" of being saved from the wrath has an unmistakable "cause," the Rapture. Thus, it is a pre-wrath Rapture of the kingdom.

This truth of a pre-wrath Rapture is confirmed by John: Those cleansed by the blood of the Lamb are in Heaven prior to God's judgment (which begins with the seventh seal).

John also makes this clear: Not a single Scripture in Revelation shows Christ's kingdom on the Earth, being saved from wrath, during the time of wrath. Without question, when the sixth seal opens, those in the kingdom will be transformed (1 Cor. 15:51–57) and transported to His throne.

This is the truth: We "wait for his Son from heaven, whom he raised from the dead—Jesus, who rescues us from the coming wrath" (1 Thess. 1:10).

With the sixth seal, the church (the mystery) is now in Heaven. This is precisely why one of Heaven's elders presents John with a rhetorical question. The elder asks: "Who are these [people] clothed in the long white robes? And from where have they come?"

John said: "Sir, you know." And he said to me, "These are they who have come out of the great tribulation (persecution), and have washed their robes and made them white in the blood of the Lamb." In other words, the mystery of this multitude is made clear for all to understand: They have been raptured out of the great tribulation on the Earth because they were cleansed by the blood of the Lamb.

Once in Heaven, those saved by the blood of the Lamb will declare the source of their salvation: God and His Son, the Lamb. Now, in the presence of God, there shall be no tribulation or condemnation, only glory. Whereas palm branches symbolize great joy and triumph, the shelter is God's righteousness, covering all who are in His presence.

In Heaven, human identities shall be retained. As each individual was known on Earth, so shall they be known in Heaven. As written by Paul, "then I shall know fully, even as I am fully known" (1 Cor. 13:12).

Paul described this coming day of the Rapture as "the day of our Lord Jesus Christ" (1 Cor. 1:8). Additionally, Paul revealed another critical detail about this day; he prophesied the kingdom will be harvested from the Earth with a divine signal: the sound of "the last trumpet."

> Listen, I tell you a mystery: We will not all sleep, but we will all be changed—in a flash, in the twinkling of an eye, at the last trumpet. For the trumpet will sound, the dead will be raised imperishable, and we will be changed. For the perishable must clothe itself with the imperishable, and the mortal with immortality. (1 Cor. 15:51–53)

"The last trumpet" sounds on a holy day, known as the Feast of Trumpets (*Rosh HaShanah*). The Feast of Trumpets begins with a celestial sign: the lunar signal of the seventh new moon on the Hebrew calendar (which typically occurs in September, which is the time of harvest). In ancient times, the temple authorities did not know the day or hour this feast would commence because this could only be decided once the seventh new moon was sighted.

The Feast of Trumpets is also referred to as the "Feast of the New Moon," for it is the only annual feast of God that commences with a lunar sign. Thus, time is marked on the Hebrew calendar. At the sound of "the last trumpet" on an unknown year during the Feast of Trumpets, our Lord will harvest His kingdom to His throne.[28]

Without debate, when the sixth seal does open, the course of history will be altered. At this time, Earth will witness divine intervention like it hasn't seen since the first century A.D. Heaven's communication to Earth will be unmistakable. For those not in Christ's kingdom, the signs of the sixth seal represent instantaneous future shock delivered without prior notification.

Paul presented a contrast between those not in Christ's kingdom (who glory in earthly treasures), and the citizens of Heaven (the King's kingdom):

> For there are many, of whom I have often told you, and now tell you even with tears, who live as enemies of the cross of Christ [rejecting and opposing His way of salvation], whose fate is destruction, whose god is their belly [their worldly appetite,

their sensuality, their vanity], and whose glory is in their shame—who focus their mind on earthly and temporal things. But [we are different, because] our citizenship is in heaven. And from there we eagerly await [the coming of] the Savior, the Lord Jesus Christ; who, by exerting that power which enables Him even to subject everything to Himself, will [not only] transform [but completely refashion] our *earthly* bodies so that they will be like His glorious *resurrected* body. (Phil. 3:18–21)

With the King's kingdom in Heaven, the stage will be set for the second coming of Christ to Israel. As John documented, years will pass between the Rapture and the second coming, but as John also documented, when Christ descends from Heaven to save Israel, He will be accompanied by His kingdom, His faithful followers.

John offered a preview of the second coming of Christ and the battle of Armageddon:

They [the ten kings] will make war against the Lamb, but the Lamb will overcome them because he is Lord of lords and King of kings—and with him will be his called, chosen and faithful followers. (Rev. 17:14)

The King's kingdom will accompany Him from Heaven at the second coming, which is when the battle of Armageddon will come to pass. John specifically called it "the battle of that great day of God Almighty" (Rev. 16:14). It is the culmination of God's great day of wrath.

Whereas the sixth seal announces the coming wrath, the seventh seal initiates it.

The Seventh Seal

When he opened the seventh seal, there was a silence in heaven for about half an hour. And I saw the seven angels who stand before God, and to them were given seven trumpets. Another angel, who had a golden censer, came and stood at the altar. He was given much incense to offer, with the prayers of all the saints, on the golden altar before the throne. The smoke of the incense, together with the prayers of the saints, went up before God from the angel's hand. Then the angel took the censer, filled it with fire from the altar, and hurled it on the earth; and there came peals of thunder, rumblings, flashes of lightning and an earthquake. (Rev. 8:1–5)

The seventh seal sends a sweeping silence throughout the heavenly realm, for like a spiritual curtain, judgment shall now descend on planet Earth. An earthquake will literally shake the remaining population as a firestorm of thunder and lightning rages overhead. With these signs, the seven angels shall sound their trumpets, and one plague after another shall befall the world.

> The first angel sounded his trumpet, and there came hail and fire mixed with blood, and it was hurled down upon the earth. A third of the earth was burned up, a third of the trees were burned up, and all the green grass was burned up. The second angel sounded his trumpet, and something like a huge mountain, all ablaze, was thrown into the sea. A third of the sea turned into blood, a third of the living creatures in the sea died, and a third of the ships were destroyed. The third angel sounded his trumpet, and a great star, blazing like a torch, fell from the sky on a third of the rivers and on the springs of water—the name of the star is Wormwood. A third of the waters turned bitter, and many people died from the waters that had become bitter. The fourth angel sounded his trumpet, and a third of the sun was struck, a third of the moon, and a third of the stars, so that a third of them turned dark. A third of the day was without light, and also a third of the night. As I watched, I heard an eagle that was flying in midair call out in a loud voice: "Woe! Woe! Woe to the inhabitants of the earth, because of the trumpet blasts about to be sounded by the other three angels!" (Rev. 8:7–13)

The plagued Earth shall resemble the days

when Moses confronted Pharaoh in Egypt and "blood was everywhere" (Exod. 7:21). As wrath poured down upon Egypt, so it will upon the world as the trumpets sound.

With the fourth angel, time is marked by an eerie darkness that fills the planet; it is the omen that wrath shall grievously intensify. When the angels release their "woes," the global effects will be unprecedented.

The fifth angel sounded his trumpet, and I saw a star that had fallen from the sky to the earth. The star was given the key to the shaft of the Abyss. When he opened the Abyss, smoke rose from it like the smoke from a gigantic furnace. The sun and sky were darkened by the smoke from the Abyss. And out of the smoke locusts came down upon the earth and were given power like that of scorpions of the earth. They were told not to harm the grass of the earth or any plant or tree, but only those people who did not have the seal of God on their foreheads. They were not given power to kill them, but only to torture them for five months. And the agony they suffered was like that of the sting of a scorpion when it strikes a man. During those days men will seek death, but will not find it; they will long to die, but death will elude them. The locusts looked like horses prepared for battle. On their heads they wore something like crowns of gold, and their faces resembled human faces. Their hair was like women's hair, and their teeth were like lions' teeth. They had breastplates like breastplates of iron, and the sound of their wings was like the thundering of many horses and chariots rushing into battle. They had tails and stings like scorpions, and in their tails they had power to torment people for five months. They had as king over them the angel of the Abyss, whose name in Hebrew is Abaddon, and in Greek, Apollyon. The first woe is past; two other woes are yet to come. (Rev. 9:1–12)

From out of the bottomless pit, a demonic horde of vicious creatures shall assault the population (sparing only the 144,000 sealed by God). Abaddon shall rise to lead the attack.

When this woe has passed, the sixth trumpet will sound.

The sixth angel sounded his trumpet, and I heard a voice coming from the horns of the golden altar that is before God. It said to the sixth angel who had the trumpet, "Release the four angels who are bound at the great river Euphrates." And the four angels who had been kept ready for this very hour and day and month and year were released to kill a third of mankind. The number of the mounted troops was two hundred million. I heard their number. The horses and riders I saw in my vision looked like this: Their breastplates were fiery red, dark blue, and yellow as sulfur. The heads of the horses resembled the heads of lions, and out of their mouths came fire, smoke and sulfur. A third of mankind was killed by the three plagues of fire, smoke and sulfur that came out of their mouths. The power of the horses was in their mouths and in their tails; for their tails were like snakes, having heads with which they inflict injury. The rest of mankind that were not killed by these plagues still did not repent of the work of their hands; they did not stop worshiping demons, and idols of gold, silver, bronze, stone and wood—idols that cannot see or hear or walk. Nor did they repent of their murders, their magic arts, their sexual immorality or their thefts. (Rev. 9:13–21)

With one third of the world's population succumbing to this judgment, the nations will be traumatized. From out of this devastation, a leader will rise to power. Eventually revealed to be the Antichrist, he will broker a seven-year peace treaty. This treaty will mark the beginning of the seven-year prophecy given by the prophet Daniel, known as the "seventieth seven."

According to John, during the first three-and-one-half years of this seven-year prophecy, two prophets of God will smite the planet with unrelenting plagues. The Antichrist will rise up, slay the two prophets, and then rule from the Holy Land with the false prophet for the next three-and-one-half years. Hence, together, the prophets of Heaven and hell make up the "seventieth seven" given by Daniel.

(Note: The "sixty-ninth seven" was fulfilled with the first coming of Christ to the Holy Land when He was crucified, or "cut off" (Dan. 9:26).) The "seventieth seven" will be fulfilled with the second coming of Christ to the Holy Land when He destroys the Antichrist and rescues Israel. The gap in time between the first and second coming of Christ was a mystery.

Christ revealed the mystery of this gap in time to Paul. In this gap, the Gospel of grace would go out to all Gentile nations. This time (which time we are in now) is known as the "times of the Gentiles" (Luke 21:24), for the Creator extended His invitation to enter His eternal kingdom to all nations so all bloodlines could become one in the temple of the living God. With the fulfillment of this prophecy (and time), God will remember Israel and save it. This is what Paul prophesied:

> For I do not desire, brethren, that you should be ignorant of this mystery, lest you should be wise in your own opinion, that blindness in part has happened to Israel until the fullness of the Gentiles has come in. And so all Israel will be saved, as it is written: "The Deliverer will come out of Zion, And He will turn away ungodliness from Jacob; For this is My covenant with them, When I take away their sins." (Rom. 11:25–27)

In the first century A.D., the nation of Israel rejected the Messiah and it remains in a state of partial blindness. However, Israel will be delivered with second coming of Christ (who is the Deliverer). (Christ Himself marked this gap in time between His first coming to Israel and His second coming to Israel; Peter did likewise.[29]) When the fullness of the Gentiles has arrived, God will save Israel and fulfill the prophecy of Daniel's "seventieth seven."

Daniel's "seventieth seven" is in actuality the seven-year countdown to the battle of Armageddon when Christ will deliver Israel from the Antichrist. Daniel's seven-year prophecy summarizes what will come to pass during this time:

> The people of the ruler [the Antichrist] who will come will destroy the city [Jerusalem] and the sanctuary. The end will come like a flood: War will continue until the end, and desolations have been decreed. He [the Antichrist] will confirm a covenant with many for one 'seven' [the seventieth]. In the middle of the 'seven' [after three-and-a-half years] he will put an end to sacrifice and offering. And on a wing of the temple he [the Antichrist] will set up an abomination that causes desolation, until the end that is decreed is poured out on him [at Armageddon]." (Dan. 9:26, 27)

The Antichrist will come in the name of peace with war in his soul. Although the Antichrist will confirm a covenant (an agreement) he will break his agreement. Three-and-one-half years into the covenant, he will kill God's prophets and end godly sacrifice and offerings.

The Antichrist will set up a talking idol, and for three-and-one-half years, the Antichrist will rule, establishing his one-world religion. However, his ill-fated attempt to control the planet will end when the Son of God and His armies will pour out destruction at the battle of Armageddon. This prophecy of the "seventieth seven" is expounded upon by John.

According to John, the seven-year prophecy commences with two prophets of God.

"And I [God] will give power to my two witnesses, and they will prophesy for 1,260 days, clothed in sackcloth." These are the two olive trees and the two lampstands that stand before the Lord of the earth. If anyone tries to harm them, fire comes from their mouths and devours their enemies. This is how anyone who wants to harm them must die. These men have power to shut up the sky so that it will not rain during the time they are prophesying; and they have power to turn the waters into blood and to strike the earth with every kind of plague as often as they want. Now when they have finished their testimony, the beast that comes up from the Abyss will attack them, and overpower and kill them. Their bodies will lie in the street of the great city, which is figuratively called Sodom and Egypt, where also their Lord was crucified. For three and a half days men from every people, tribe, language and nation will gaze on their bodies and refuse them burial. The inhabitants of the earth will gloat over them and will celebrate by sending each other gifts, because these two prophets had tormented those who live on the earth. But after the three and a half days a breath of life from God entered them, and they stood on their feet, and terror struck those who saw them. Then they heard a loud voice from heaven saying to them, "Come up here." And they went up to heaven in a cloud, while their enemies looked on. At that very hour there was a severe earthquake and a tenth of the city collapsed. Seven thousand people were killed in the earthquake, and the survivors were terrified and gave glory to the God of heaven. The second woe has passed; the third woe is coming soon. (Rev. 11:3–14)

These prophets shall strike the unrepentant survivors with plagues as often as they command. Yet, like Christ, they shall be killed. The Antichrist shall end their lives and their plagues. He will parade their dead bodies through the streets of the dark city (now called "Sodom and Egypt"), and the evil inhabitants will find their "salvation" in the false savior.

With the death and ascension of the prophets, the globe is now on the cusp of a new order—world domination by the Antichrist. However, before John witnessed the vision of this final woe, he saw the Ark of the Covenant in the temple of God.

> Then God's temple in heaven was opened, and within his temple was seen the ark of his covenant. And there came flashes of lightning, rumblings, peals of thunder, an earthquake and a great hailstorm. (Rev. 11:19)

Upon seeing the source of all righteousness, John then witnessed the signs that mark complete unrighteousness—the third woe, the rise of the Antichrist.

The Antichrist

> And I saw a beast [the Antichrist] coming out of the sea. He had ten horns and seven heads, with ten crowns on his horns, and on each head a blasphemous name. The beast I saw resembled a leopard, but had feet like those of a bear and a mouth like that of a lion. The dragon [Satan] gave the beast his power and his throne and great authority. One of the heads of the beast seemed to have had a fatal wound, but the fatal wound had

been healed. The whole world was astonished and followed the beast. Men worshiped the dragon because he had given authority to the beast, and they also worshiped the beast and asked, "Who is like the beast? Who can make war against him?" The beast was given a mouth to utter proud words and blasphemies and to exercise his authority for forty-two months. He opened his mouth to blaspheme God, and to slander his name and his dwelling place and those who live in heaven. He was given power to make war with the saints and to conquer them. And he was given authority over every tribe, people, language and nation. All inhabitants of the earth will worship the beast—all whose names have not been written in the book of life belonging to the Lamb that was slain from the creation of the world. (Rev. 13:1–8)

Through deceit and spiritual power, the false savior shall bring order to the spiritually dark planet. This counterfeit Christ shall unite the deceived population, consolidating all secular and religious power under his hand. The darkest impulses of demonic passion shall be demonstrated without limits by a soul lost to Satan. Infused with spiritual energy, the beast shall recover from a mortal wound and deify himself.

As supreme dictator, the Antichrist will rule from his temple, proclaiming himself to be God.

> He [the Antichrist] will oppose and will exalt himself over everything that is called God or is worshiped, so that he sets himself up in God's temple, proclaiming himself to be God. The coming of the lawless one [the Antichrist] will be in accordance with the work of Satan displayed in all kinds of counterfeit miracles, signs and wonders, and in every sort of evil that deceives those who are perishing. They perish because they refused to love the truth and so be saved. (2 Thess. 2:4, 9, 10)

Through the use of "counterfeit miracles," the "lawless one" will successfully deceive the population because they "refused to love the truth."

As disciples of the Antichrist, the subservient population shall also be in subjection to the second beast. Known as the false prophet, this mouthpiece for Satan will establish and enforce the one-world religion.

The False Prophet

> Then I [John] saw another beast, coming out of the earth. He had two horns like a lamb, but he spoke like a dragon. He exercised all the authority of the first beast on his behalf, and made the earth and its inhabitants worship the first beast, whose fatal wound

had been healed. And he performed great and miraculous signs, even causing fire to come down from heaven to earth in full view of men. Because of the signs he was given power to do on behalf of the first beast, he deceived the inhabitants of the earth. He ordered them to set up an image in honor of the beast who was wounded by the sword and yet lived. He was given power to give breath to the image of the first beast, so that it could speak and cause all who refused to worship the image to be killed. He also forced everyone, small and great, rich and poor, free and slave, to receive a mark on his right hand or on his forehead, so that no one could buy or sell unless he had the mark, which is the name of the beast or the number of his name. This calls for wisdom. If anyone has insight, let him calculate the number of the beast, for it is man's number. His number is 666. (Rev. 13:11–18)

When the population bends its knee to a talking idol and worships the Antichrist as God, Satan will deceive without restraint.

Allured by illusion, souls on Earth will relinquish their hearts to darkness and their minds to the religious order. Satan's worldwide inquisition shall produce martyrs or abject servitude. Those who choose to make a covenant with Satan shall be sealed with a permanent seal, branded with the number of the beast's name: "666." Thereby, their fate cannot be altered.

Three Prophetic Visions

At this time in the chronology of Revelation, Christ reveals to John three different groups of people, all of whom are on the Earth at the time of the Antichrist: the 144,000 of the twelve tribes sealed from the wrath, those who will oppose the Antichrist, and those who will worship the Antichrist. Additionally, Christ revealed to John three prophetic visions, revealing the ultimate fates for each of the three groups. Each vision is a harvest, revealing what shall come to pass at the end of the Antichrist's reign. Thus, the harvests are prophetic in nature (concerning the future).

In one "vision," John sees those who worship the beast.

> If anyone worships the beast and his image and receives his mark on the forehead or on the hand, he, too, will drink of the wine of God's fury, which has been poured full strength into the cup of his wrath. He will be tormented with burning sulfur in the presence of the holy angels and of the Lamb. And the smoke of their torment rises for ever and ever. There is no rest day or night for those who worship the beast and his image, or for anyone who receives the mark of his name. (Rev. 14:9–11)

In a vision, John saw their ultimate fate: God will send an angel to reap the Earth.

> Another angel came out of the temple in heaven, and he too had a sharp sickle. Still another angel, who had charge of the fire, came from the altar and called in a loud voice to him who had the sharp sickle, "Take your sharp sickle and gather the clusters of grapes from the earth's vine, because its grapes are ripe." The angel swung his sickle on the earth, gathered its grapes and threw them into the great winepress of God's wrath. They were trampled in the winepress outside the city, and blood flowed out of the press, rising as high as the horses' bridles for a distance of 1,600 stadia. (Rev. 14:17–20)

This reaping contains obvious symbolism: blood doesn't flow from grapes, but it does flow from unjust and evil mankind at the battle of Armageddon. Christ reveals that this reaping of the Earth is a prophecy (a foregone conclusion). In other words, it is a prophetic vision of what shall be.

This reaping does not happen when the Antichrist rises to power, but will come to pass when he falls from power. For, it is then, at the battle of Armageddon, that the blood will flow "out of the press, rising as high as the horses' bridles for a distance of 1,600 stadia." Sixteen-hundred stadia "is approximately the length of the Holy Land from north to south."[30]   The "winepress" of God's wrath is the fulfillment of Old Testament prophecy when Christ descends from Heaven with His warriors. Joel foretold of this day:

> Bring down your warriors, Lord! "Let the nations be roused; let them advance into the Valley of Jehoshaphat, for there I will sit to judge all the nations on every side. Swing the sickle, for the harvest is ripe. Come, trample the grapes, for the winepress is full and the vats overflow—so great is their wickedness!" Multitudes, multitudes in the valley of decision! For the day of the Lord is near in the valley of decision. The sun and moon will be darkened, and the stars no longer shine. The Lord will roar from Zion and thunder from Jerusalem; the earth and the heavens will tremble. But the Lord will be a refuge for his people, a stronghold for the people of Israel. (Joel 3:11–16)

This judgment at Armageddon (and deliverance of Israel) will come to pass at the second coming of Christ. In John's prophetic vision, those who worship the Antichrist shall end up in God's winepress, crushed.

In another prophetic vision, John sees those who do not worship the Antichrist, but rather, turn to Christ:

> Then I heard a voice from heaven say, "Write this: Blessed are the dead who die in

the Lord from now on." "Yes," says the Spirit, "they will rest from their labor, for their deeds will follow them." (Rev. 14:13)

Those who "die in the Lord from now on" refers to those who die from the beginning of the Antichrist's reign to the end of it. These martyrs will be blessed and resurrected. Thus, this group is victorious over the beast. John, in a prophetic vision, sees their ultimate glory:

And I saw what looked like a sea of glass glowing with fire and, standing beside the sea, those who had been victorious over the beast and its image and over the number of its name. They held harps given them by God and sang the song of God's servant Moses and of the Lamb: "Great and marvelous are your deeds, Lord God Almighty. Just and true are your ways, King of the nations. Who will not fear you, Lord, and bring glory to your name? For you alone are holy. All nations will come and worship before you, for your righteous acts have been revealed." (Rev. 15:2–4)

Those who sing this song are those who "die in the Lord." The resurrection of the martyrs is a prophetic vision, which shall come to pass after the destruction of the Antichrist (Revelation 20:4).

For the third group—the 144,000—John sees this:

Then I looked, and there before me was the Lamb, standing on Mount Zion, and with him 144,000 who had his name and his Father's name written on their foreheads. And I heard a sound from heaven like the roar of rushing waters and like a loud peal of thunder. The sound I heard was like that of harpists playing their harps. And they sang a new song before the throne and before the four living creatures and the elders. No one could learn the song except the 144,000 who had been redeemed from the earth. These are those who did not defile themselves with women, for they remained virgins. They follow the Lamb wherever he goes. They were purchased from among mankind and offered as first fruits to God and the Lamb. No lie was found in their mouths; they are blameless. (Rev. 14:1–5)

In the corresponding prophetic vision, John sees this:

I looked, and there before me was a white cloud, and seated on the cloud was one like a son of man with a crown of gold on his head and a sharp sickle in his hand. Then another angel came out of the temple and called in a loud voice to him who was sitting on the cloud, "Take your sickle and reap, because the time to reap has come, for the harvest of the earth is ripe." So he who was seated on the cloud swung his sickle over the earth, and the earth was harvested. (Rev. 14:14–16)

The 144,000 are the "first fruits" of Israel, which shall be reaped from the Earth at the same time as the other two harvests: at the fall of the Antichrist.

The harvest of the 144,000 sets the stage for the full resurrection of the twelve tribes of Israel; the timing of this resurrection is unmistakable. It follows the destruction of the Antichrist and will fulfill God's promise given to Daniel (Dan.11:45; 12:1–3).

Prior to the fulfillment of the three prophetic visions, the seven angels will unleash the final seven plagues.

The Final Seven Plagues

I [John] saw in heaven another great and marvelous sign: seven angels with the seven last plagues—last, because with them God's wrath is completed. Then I heard a loud voice from the temple saying to the seven angels, "Go, pour out the seven bowls of God's wrath on the earth."

The first angel went and poured out his bowl on the land, and ugly and painful sores broke out on the people who had the mark of the beast and worshiped his image.

The second angel poured out his bowl on the sea, and it turned into blood like that of a dead man, and every living thing in the sea died.

The third angel poured out his bowl on the rivers and springs of water, and they became blood. Then I heard the angel in charge of the waters say: "You are just in these judgments, you who are and who were, the Holy One, because you have so judged; for they have shed the blood of your saints and prophets, and you have given them blood to drink as they deserve." And I heard the altar respond: "Yes, Lord God Almighty, true and just are your judgments."

The fourth angel poured out his bowl on the sun, and the sun was given power to scorch people with fire. They were seared by the intense heat and they cursed the name of God, who had control over these plagues, but they refused to repent and glorify him.

The fifth angel poured out his bowl on the throne of the beast, and his kingdom was plunged into darkness. Men gnawed their tongues in agony and cursed the God of heaven because of their pains and their sores, but they refused to repent of what they had done.

The sixth angel poured out his bowl on the great river Euphrates, and its water was dried up to prepare the way for the kings from the East. Then I saw three evil spirits that looked like frogs; they came out of the mouth of the dragon, out of the mouth of the beast and out of the mouth of the false prophet. They are spirits of demons performing miraculous signs, and they go out to the kings of the whole world, to gather them for the battle on the great day of God Almighty. Then they gathered the kings together to the place that in Hebrew is called Armageddon. (Rev. 15:1; 16:1–14, 16)

With the evaporation of the Euphrates River, the kings of the East will sweep into the Middle East to Armageddon. ("Armageddon is a compound word that means 'mountain of Megiddo.' All major traffic through northern Palestine traveled past Megiddo, making it a strategic military stronghold."[31]) Like every evil army that has cursed the globe, however, these warriors are nothing more than pawns on the chessboard, wasted souls without hope. Divine prophecy is against them.

Then the Lord will go out and fight against those nations, as he fights on a day of battle. On that day his feet will stand on the Mount of Olives, east of Jerusalem, and the Mount of Olives will be split in two from east to west, forming a great valley, with half of the mountain moving north and half moving south. Then the Lord my God will come, and all the holy ones with him. (Zech. 14:3–5)

When this prophecy comes to pass, the King will descend from Heaven with His holy ones— "his called, chosen and faithful followers" (Rev.

17:14). The King of kings will obliterate ten of Satan's kings. No armament made in this world will be able to withstand the power that Christ shall bring from Heaven. At the battle of Armageddon, the true Christ shall annihilate the children of darkness, forever separating them from the glory and strength of Almighty God.

> [T]he Lord Jesus shall be revealed from heaven with his mighty angels, In flaming fire taking vengeance on them that know not God, and that obey not the gospel of our Lord Jesus Christ: Who shall be punished with everlasting destruction from the presence of the Lord, and from the glory of his power. (2 Thess. 1:7–9)

This prophecy marks the culmination of the day of the Lord, when the Lord Jesus Christ will be "revealed" (Greek: *Apokalupso*[32]). The "Apocalypse" (derived from *Apokalupso*) is associated with Christ's second coming to Israel and the battle of Armageddon. (In his prophecy about the Apocalypse, Paul states the church should not be concerned about this, or "shaken" (2 Thess. 2:2), as the Rapture will occur before the Apocalypse.[33])

When the Son of God prophesied of the Apocalypse, He compared it to the horrific destruction that fell upon Sodom and Gomorrah:

> It was the same in the days of Lot. People were eating and drinking, buying and

selling, planting and building. But the day Lot left Sodom, fire and sulfur rained down from heaven and destroyed them all. It will be just like this on the day the Son of Man is revealed. (Luke 17:28–30)

Just as the unsuspecting inhabitants of the morally bankrupt cities reaped the consequences of their actions, so shall those in the Antichrist's kingdom at the Apocalypse.

When Christ prophesied of the Apocalypse, He said: "Behold, I come like a thief!" (Rev. 16:15). This prophecy is in the context of Armageddon, which is "the battle on the great day of God Almighty" (Rev. 16:14).

This prophecy of a "thief" has a precedent. Isaiah prophesied of Israel's salvation and how that salvation would be instantaneous and dramatic.

But the multitude of your enemies [that assault you] will become like fine dust, And the multitude of the tyrants like the chaff which blows away; And it will happen in an instant, suddenly [that your enemy is destroyed]. You will be punished by the Lord of hosts with thunder and earthquake and great noise, With whirlwind and tempest and the flame of a consuming fire. (Isa. 29:5, 6)

Isaiah spoke of time and marked dramatic signs that shall accompany the second coming of

Christ when He returns "like a thief." Herein, Christ's reference to a thief speaks not of a quiet return, but of the sudden surprise of His return. Additionally, those who are in spiritual darkness will be overtaken, and those who embrace spiritual light are commanded to "watch" (Rev. 16:15). (This is precisely how Paul used the expression of a "thief" to describe the Rapture (1 Thess. 5:2).)

Christ (and His armies) will descend like a thief after the seventh angel smites the planet with the final plague.

> The seventh angel poured out his bowl into the air, and out of the temple came a loud voice from the throne, saying, "It is done!" Then there came flashes of lightning, rumblings, peals of thunder and a severe earthquake. No earthquake like it has ever occurred since man has been on earth, so tremendous was the quake. The great city split into three parts, and the cities of the nations collapsed. God remembered Babylon the Great and gave her the cup filled with the wine of the fury of his wrath. Every island fled away and the mountains could not be found. From the sky huge hailstones of about a hundred pounds each fell upon men. And they cursed God on account of the plague of hail, because the plague was so terrible. (Rev. 16:17–21)

With thunder and lightning saturating the

sky, a catastrophic earthquake will send fissures rippling throughout the planet. Every island shall slide into the sea, and mountain ranges shall collapse. With his empire literally crumbling, the Antichrist will witness his capital split in three directions. Earth itself shall tear at the very foundation of his throne.

The inhabitants marked by the beast are trapped in the world they conquered. While they are being bombarded with hail stones, the pitiful survivors will shake their fists at God, blaming Him instead of placing blame where it belongs— on themselves and their wickedness.

This cataclysmic event marks time. The Apocalypse is at the door. Christ will descend out of Heaven and shall be victorious, when the armies of Heaven fight against the armies of Earth.

The Apocalypse

I [John] saw heaven standing open and there before me was a white horse whose rider is called Faithful and True. With justice he judges and makes war. His eyes are like blazing fire, and on his head are many crowns. He has a name written on him that no one knows but himself. He is dressed in a robe dipped in blood, and his name is the Word of God. The armies of heaven were following him, riding on white horses and dressed in fine linen, white and clean. Out of his mouth came a sharp sword with which to strike down the nations. "He will rule them with an iron scepter." He treads the winepress of the fury of the wrath of God Almighty. On his robe and on his thigh he has this name written: KING OF KINGS AND LORD OF LORDS.

And I saw an angel standing in the sun, who cried in a loud voice to all the birds flying in midair, "Come, gather together for the great supper of God, so that you may eat the flesh of kings, generals, and mighty men, of horses and their riders, and the flesh of all people, free and slave, small and great." Then I saw the beast and the kings of the earth and their armies gathered together to make war against the rider on the horse and his army. But the beast was captured, and with him the false prophet who had performed the miraculous signs on his behalf. With these signs he had deluded those who had received the mark of the beast and worshiped his image. The two of them were thrown alive into the fiery lake of burning sulfur. The rest of them were killed with the sword that came out of the mouth of the rider on the horse, and all the birds gorged themselves on their flesh. (Rev. 19:11–21)

God's King will overtake Satan's "king." As Moses delivered the Israelites from the hand of

Pharaoh, so will Christ deliver remnants of the twelve tribes from the grip of the Antichrist (and gather them back to the Holy Land). This is precisely what Jesus prophesied while in the Holy Land:

> For then there will be great distress, unequaled from the beginning of the world until now—and never to be equaled again. If those days had not been cut short, no one would survive, but for the sake of the elect those days will be shortened. Immediately after the tribulation of those days shall the sun be darkened, and the moon shall not give her light, and the stars shall fall from heaven, and the powers of the heavens shall be shaken: and then shall appear the sign of the Son of man in heaven: and then shall all the tribes of the earth mourn, and they shall see the Son of man coming in the clouds of heaven with power and great glory. And he shall send his angels with a great sound of a trumpet, and they shall gather together his elect from the four winds, from one end of heaven to the other. (Matt. 24:21, 22, 29–31)

When the sun turns dark and the moon is dark (not blood red), the Son of God will descend from the right hand of God to the Holy Land. With the sound of the great trumpet, the Messiah will gather the "elect."

Who is the elect? It is defined by the context within which the word is used, because elect can mean the church of God, or it can mean "Israel mine elect" (Isa. 45:4).

Jesus was sent to "the lost sheep of the house of Israel" (Matt. 15:24). His prophecy to gather the elect builds upon prophecies already spoken by the prophets sent to Israel, including Moses and Isaiah.

Moses prophesied:

[T]hen the Lord your God will restore your fortunes and have compassion on you and gather you again from all the nations where he scattered you. Even if you have been banished to the most distant land under the heavens, from there the Lord your God will gather you and bring you back. He will bring you to the land that belonged to your ancestors, and you will take possession of it. He will make you more prosperous and numerous than your ancestors. The Lord your God will circumcise your hearts and the hearts of your descendants, so that you may love him with all your heart and with all your soul, and live. (Deut. 30:3–6)

Isaiah prophesied:

And it shall come to pass in that day, that the Lord shall beat off from the channel of the river unto the stream of Egypt, and ye shall be gathered one by one, O ye children of Israel. And it shall come to pass in that day, that the great trumpet shall be blown, and they shall come which were ready to perish in the land of Assyria, and the outcasts in the land of Egypt, and shall worship the Lord in the holy mount at Jerusalem. (Isa. 27:12, 13)

At the sound of "the great trumpet"[34] (not "the last trumpet"), the Messiah will deliver and gather Israel. (The great trumpet sounds at the time of the Apocalypse and the last trumpet sounds at the time of the Rapture.)

Israel's Judgment

These prophecies of the second coming to Israel and the gathering of Israel back to the Holy Land will set the stage for a resurrection and judgment of Israel. It is then that Daniel's prophecy about Israel's deliverance, resurrection, and judgment will be fulfilled:

At that time Michael, the great prince who protects your people, will arise. There will be a time of distress such as has not happened from the beginning of nations until then. But at that time your people—everyone whose name is found written in the book—will be delivered. Multitudes who sleep in the dust of the earth will awake: some to everlasting life, others to shame and everlasting contempt. Those who are wise will shine like the brightness of the heavens, and those who lead many to righteousness, like the stars for ever and ever. (Dan. 12:1–3)

At this judgment, everyone of Daniel's people (Israel) whose name is found written in the book will be delivered.

The timing of this judgment is unmistakable. Daniel said there is a unique time on Earth that precedes it: "There will be a time of distress such as has not happened from the beginning of nations until then." It is the same unique time prophesied by Jeremiah: "Alas! for that day is great, so that none is like it: it is even the time of Jacob's trouble, but he shall be saved out of it" (Jer. 30:7). This is the time of Jacob's trouble (not the church's trouble). Yet, Israel (the elect) will be saved out of it. This is precisely what Jesus prophesied:

For then there will be great tribulation, such as has not been since the beginning of the world until this time, no, nor ever shall be. And unless those days were shortened, no flesh would be saved; but for the elect's sake those days will be shortened. (Matt. 24:21, 22)

This time of great tribulation is the unique time of wrath that precedes the Apocalypse, which precedes the judgment of the twelve tribes.

Christ Himself prophesied of this coming

judgment of Israel, and how the apostles will judge the twelve tribes:

> Jesus said to them, "Truly I tell you, at the renewal of all things, when the Son of Man sits on his glorious throne, you who have followed me will also sit on twelve thrones, judging the twelve tribes of Israel." (Matt. 19:28)

The second coming to Israel is the time judgment, but it is also the time of renewal and cleansing.

Of the many prophecies that refer to the second coming of Christ to the Holy Land, one given by the prophet Ezekiel makes specific reference to the priestly responsibility that takes place on the sixth holy day, the Day of Atonement *(Yom Kippur)*. God prophesied of Israel's gathering and cleansing:

> For I will take you out of the nations; I will gather you from all the countries and bring you back into your own land. I will sprinkle clean water on you, and you will be clean; I will cleanse you from all your impurities and from all your idols. I will give you a new heart and put a new spirit in you; I will remove from you your heart of stone and give you a heart of flesh. And I will put my Spirit in you and move you to follow my decrees and be careful to keep my laws. Then you will live in the land I gave your

ancestors; you will be my people, and I will be your God. (Ezek. 36:24–28)

Today, the Son of God reigns as the great high priest in Heaven. He will return to the Holy Land as Lord, King, and priest to deliver, to gather, to judge, to cleanse, and to make atonement. This will mark the fulfillment of the Day of Atonement. And this time of atonement is the time of renewal. From the ashes of Armageddon, a new thousand-year kingdom shall rise upon the Earth: the millennial kingdom. For one thousand years, the Son of God will reign over the world from Jerusalem.

The Millennial Kingdom

In a vision, John saw those martyred under the beast, who will reign with Christ.

I saw the souls of those who had been beheaded because of their testimony for Jesus and because of the word of God. They had not worshiped the beast or his image and had not received his mark on their foreheads or their hands. They came to life and reigned with Christ a thousand years. (The rest of the dead did not come to life until the thousand years were ended.) This is the first resurrection. Blessed and holy are those who have part in the first resurrection. The second death has no power over them, but they will be priests of God and of Christ and will reign with him for a thousand years. (Rev. 20:4–6)

Following the resurrections, the Creator will "restore the fortunes of Judah and Jerusalem" (Joel 3:1). It is then that the millennial kingdom will commence. The Lord God Himself prophesied of this coming, glorious time:

Then you will know that I, the Lord your God, dwell in Zion, my holy hill. Jerusalem will be holy; never again will foreigners invade her. In that day the mountains will drip new wine, and the hills will flow with milk; all the ravines of Judah will run with water. (Joel 3:17, 18)

Of this magnificent day, God proclaimed:

I will return to Zion, And dwell in the midst of Jerusalem. Jerusalem shall be called the City of Truth, The Mountain of the Lord of hosts, The Holy Mountain. (Zech. 8:3)

And many nations of the Earth will say:

"Come, and let us go up to the mountain of the Lord, To the house of the God of Jacob; He will teach us His ways, And we shall walk in His paths." For out of Zion the law shall go forth, And the word of the Lord from Jerusalem. He shall judge between many peoples, And rebuke strong nations afar off; They shall beat their swords into plowshares, And their spears into pruning hooks; Nation shall not lift up sword against nation, Neither shall they learn war anymore. But everyone shall sit under his vine and under his fig tree, And no one shall make *them* afraid; For the mouth of the Lord of hosts has spoken. (Micah 4:2–4)

God has spoken and He will fulfill: God's Son will bring Heaven on Earth, reigning in righteousness.

He will be great, and will be called the Son of the Highest; and the Lord God will give Him the throne of His father David. And He will reign over the house of Jacob forever, and of His kingdom there will be no end. (Luke 1:32, 33)

Of the greatness of his government and peace there will be no end. He will reign on David's throne and over his kingdom, establishing and upholding it with justice and righteousness from that time on and forever. The zeal of the Lord Almighty will accomplish this. (Isa. 9:7)

This unprecedented time of peace on Earth will usher in the fulfillment of the seventh and final holy day: the Festival of Tabernacles (*Sukkot*). All nations will celebrate it, annually.

As Zechariah prophesied:

> Then the survivors from all the nations that have attacked Jerusalem will go up year after year to worship the King, the Lord Almighty, and to celebrate the Festival of Tabernacles. (Zech. 14:16)

The Festival of Tabernacles calls to memory the time the children of Israel lived in the desert (the wilderness) in temporary dwellings following the Exodus from Egypt. In the desert, God dwelled with them. God told Moses: "have them make a sanctuary for me, and I will dwell among them" (Exod. 25:8). The Festival of Tabernacles, which lasted for seven days, foreshadowed God dwelling with all His people during the millennial kingdom.

During this time of unprecedented peace on Earth, Satan will be imprisoned in the bottomless pit.

> And I saw an angel coming down out of heaven, having the key to the Abyss and holding in his hand a great chain. He seized the dragon, that ancient serpent, who is the devil, or Satan, and bound him for a thousand years. He threw him into the Abyss, and locked and sealed it over him, to keep him from deceiving the nations anymore until the thousand years were ended. After that, he must be set free for a short time. (Rev. 20:1–3)

With the dark angel imprisoned in the pit, the world will experience life without Satan's deception. Yet, this separation between righteousness and unrighteousness is only temporary, for Satan will be released from his shackles and will pursue one last attempt to destroy God's people. His final move against God, however, brings checkmate.

The Final Conflict

> When the thousand years are over, Satan will be released from his prison and will go out to deceive the nations in the four corners of the earth—Gog and Magog—to gather them for battle. In number they are like the sand on the seashore. They marched across the breadth of the earth and surrounded the camp of God's people, the city he loves. But fire came down from heaven and devoured them. And the devil, who deceived them, was thrown into the lake of burning sulfur, where the beast and the false prophet had been thrown. They will be tormented day and night for ever and ever. (Rev. 20:7–10)

In the lake of fire, Satan shall remember God's justice forever. The calamity he brought upon creation shall be upon him without end.

His army shall know immediate death. Called "Gog and Magog" because it is the embodiment of ancient evil, the army shall fall to the will of Heaven, the evil it brought shall be forever expunged, and divine prophecy will be fulfilled (Ezek. 38).

Following this threshold in time, another resurrection of the seventh seal will come to pass. All souls not raised during the previous resurrections shall be judged.

The Final Judgment

> Then I saw a great white throne and him who was seated on it. Earth and sky fled from his presence, and there was no place for them. And I saw the dead, great and small, standing before the throne, and books were opened. Another book was opened, which is the book of life. The dead were judged according to what they had done as recorded in the books. The sea gave up the dead that were in it, and death and Hades gave up the dead that were in them, and each person was judged according to what he had done. Then death and Hades were thrown into the lake of fire. The lake of fire is the second death. If anyone's name was not found written in the book of life, he was thrown into the lake of fire. (Rev. 20:11–15)

From the center of the Great White Throne, Christ shall judge. Those souls who are "blotted out of the book of life and not listed with the righteous" (Ps. 69:28), will die a second death. Never shall their souls live again. In contrast, any soul found in the book of life shall live to see paradise.

Christ Himself prophesied of this Day of Judgment:

> When the Son of Man comes in his glory, and all the angels with him, he will sit on his glorious throne. All the nations will be gathered before him, and he will separate the people one from another as a shepherd separates the sheep from the goats. He will put the sheep on his right and the goats on his left. Then the King will say to those on his right, "Come, you who are blessed by my Father; take your inheritance, the kingdom prepared for you since the creation of the world." Then he will say to those on his left, "Depart from me, you who are cursed, into the eternal fire prepared for the devil and his angels." (Matt. 25:31–34, 41)

This is the end: the permanent separation of light from darkness. Desperation awaits those who are sentenced to the "second death," whereas unlimited love and freedom await the righteous. This prophecy of judgment marks not only the permanent divide between Heaven and hell, but also the transition between this world and the next.

The New Heaven and New Earth

Lift up your eyes to the heavens, look at the earth beneath; the heavens will vanish like smoke, the earth will wear out like a garment. (Isa. 51:6)

[W]e look for new heavens and a new earth according to His promise, in which righteousness (uprightness, freedom from sin, and right standing with God) is to abide. (2 Peter 3:13)

The former things will not be remembered, nor will they come to mind. (Isa. 65:17)

As presented in Chapter 5 of this book, visions of this new creation—the most intriguing scenes ever revealed—were given to John. His opening vision is revisited here:

Then I saw a new sky (heaven) and a new earth, for the former sky and the former earth had passed away (vanished), and there no longer existed any sea. And I saw the holy city, the new Jerusalem, descending out of heaven from God, all arrayed like a bride beautified and adorned for her husband; Then I heard a mighty voice from the throne and I perceived its distinct words, saying, See! The abode of God is with men, and He will live (encamp, tent) among them; and they shall be His people, and God shall personally be with them and be their God. God will wipe away every tear from their eyes; and death shall be no more, neither shall there be anguish (sorrow and mourning) nor grief nor pain any more, for the old conditions and the former order of things have passed away. And He Who is seated on the throne said, See! I make all things new. Also He said, Record this, for these sayings are faithful (accurate, incorruptible, and trustworthy) and true (genuine). And He [further] said to me, It is done! I am the Alpha and the Omega, the Beginning and the End. To the thirsty I [Myself] will give water without price from the fountain (springs) of the water of Life. He who is victorious shall inherit all these things, and I will be God to him and he shall be My son. (Rev. 21:1–7)

In this new world, space and time will be redefined. Time's marking will expand beyond human comprehension. "With the Lord a day is like a thousand years, and a thousand years are like a day" (2 Peter 3:8). No longer will time reflect the placement of the sun, moon, and stars because no sun will exist to light the new Earth; God's glorious majesty will illuminate it.

Eternal souls will continue forward in an elevated state of awareness, in a permanent state of peace. Christ prophesied of this coming age, contrasting it with our current age:

The people of this age marry, and are given in marriage. But those who are considered worthy of taking part in that age and in the resurrection from the dead, will neither marry nor be given in marriage, and they can no longer die; for they are like the angels. They are God's children, since they are children of the resurrection. (Luke 20:34–36)

Now, enjoy Christ's final revelation to John regarding our coming paradise:

Then the angel showed me the river of the water of life, as clear as crystal, flowing from the throne of God and of the Lamb down the middle of the great street of the city. On each side of the river stood the tree of life, bearing twelve crops of fruit, yielding its fruit every month. And the leaves of the tree are for the healing of the nations. No longer will there be any curse. The throne of God and of the Lamb will be in the city, and his servants will serve him. They will see his face, and his name will be on their foreheads. There will be no more night. They will not need the light of a lamp or the light of the sun, for the Lord God will give them light. And they will reign for ever and ever. The angel said to me, "These words are trustworthy and true. The Lord, the God who inspires the prophets, sent his angel to show his servants the things that must soon take place." "Look, I am coming soon! Blessed is the one who keeps the words of the prophecy written in this scroll." (Rev. 22:1–7)

The wise shall inherit glory, But shame shall be the legacy of fools. (Prov. 3:35)

Revelation: Timeline

7 Seals (Rev. 5:1–5)

1st, 2nd, 3rd, 4th Seals: The Four Horsemen (Rev. 6:1–8)

5th Seal: The Martyrs (Rev. 6:9–11)

6th Seal: Celestial and Earthly Signs (Rev. 6:12–14)

The Day of the Lord (1 Thess. 5:2)/The Great Day of His Wrath (Rev. 6:17)

a. Gentiles: Hide (Rev. 6:15–17)

b. 12 Tribes (144,000): Sealed (Rev. 7:1–8)

c. Christ's Kingdom: Raptured (Rev. 7:9–17) & Judged (1 Cor. 3:11–15)

7th Seal: Prelude to Wrath (Rev. 8:1–5)

7 Trumpets: Wrath (Rev. 8:6)

1st Trumpet: Vegetation Struck (Rev. 8:7)

2nd Trumpet: Seas Struck (Rev. 8:8, 9)

3rd Trumpet: Waters Struck (Rev. 8:10, 11)

4th Trumpet: Heavens Struck (Rev. 8:12, 13)

5th Trumpet/1st Woe: Locusts (Rev. 9:1–12)

6th Trumpet/2nd Woe: 4 Angels (Rev. 9:13–21)

"Seventieth Seven": First 3.5 years Fulfilled: God's 2 Witnesses (Rev. 11:3–14)

7th Trumpet/3rd Woe (Rev. 11:14–18)

"Seventieth Seven": Second 3.5 years Commence: Antichrist (Rev. 13:1–18)

227

7 Bowls: Wrath (Rev. 16:1)

1st Bowl: Sores upon Mankind (Rev. 16:2)

2nd Bowl: Blood Seas (Rev. 16:3)

3rd Bowl: Blood Waters (Rev. 16:4–7)

4th Bowl: Sun's Scorching Heat (Rev. 16:8, 9)

5th Bowl: Darkness (Rev. 16:10, 11)

6th Bowl: Armageddon Preparation (Rev. 16:12–16)

7th Bowl: Earthquake & Hail (Rev. 16:17–21)

The Second Coming of Christ (Rev. 19:11–21); Antichrist Defeated & "Seventieth Seven" Fulfilled (Rev. 19:21); Israel Gathered (Matt. 24:29–31) & Judged (Dan. 12:1–3)

The End

Creation, Theory and Prophecy

Not everything that can be counted counts,
and not everything that counts can be counted.
—Albert Einstein

T he history of mankind identifies a
fascination with prophecies and life in
the hereafter. As intelligent life, we
have a conscious awareness of our past and
present, but do we have a future that extends
beyond death? No question on Earth has
received more attention. Whether embracing life
after death, or accepting no exit from this world,
the question remains central to all philosophies
and religions. Even if one dismisses the
existence of life on the other side, the question of
one's real purpose in this life requires an answer.
Ironically, an honest pursuit to find one's
destiny invariably leads straight back to a
familiar thought: Why are we here in the first
place?

The answer is divided along two lines: Either
there is a divine purpose for the Earth or there

229

isn't. We are simply passing through history, or history is being made through us in the form of a greater, supernatural purpose.

Fundamentally, we all seek the obvious: love, belonging, and a sense of worth that satisfies the soul. Whether we are a success or a failure in these vital areas of life is determined by our beliefs. What we believe determines what we become. Our response as intelligent human beings should be only to take great care in determining our personal convictions.

Unfortunately, the history of man has demonstrated that beliefs—be they personal or societal—are too often based on speculation and false information and not on scientific fact, or an underlying, inherent truth. In the seventeenth century, the famous astronomer Galileo said that Earth revolved around the sun and was arrested for it. His evidence contradicted existing theory, and the "establishment" didn't like it. In essence, that moment in time represented the struggle that has saturated recorded history: the forces that seek enlightenment and the forces that seek to extinguish it.

When it comes to explaining the origin of life, no two theories are more opposed to each other than "creation" and "evolution." Whereas creationists believe that supernatural intelligence created life as we know it, evolutionists contend that life originated from single-cell organisms, which evolved into modern-day species. Hence, together, these two theories give us the opposites:

Creation and evolution, between them, exhaust the possible explanations for the origin of living things. Organisms either appeared on the earth fully developed or they did not. If they did not, they must have developed from pre-existing species by some process of modification. If they did appear in a fully developed state, they must have been created by some omnipotent intelligence.[35]

Charles Darwin promoted the idea that supernatural intelligence played no role in man's creation, and "it was because Darwinian Theory broke man's link with God and set him adrift in a cosmos without purpose or end that its impact was so fundamental. No other intellectual revolution in modern times so profoundly affected the way men viewed themselves and their place in the universe."[36]

In the year 1838, Charles Darwin lit the match that gave birth to evolutionary theory. In that year, he recorded the following statement in his notes: "Man in his arrogance thinks himself a great work. worthy [sic] the interposition of a deity, more humble & I believe true to consider him created from animals."[37]

Darwin held to the belief that man's arrogance produced creation theory. He contended that it was much more reasonable to assume that mankind evolved into its current state. In his publication, *On the Origin of Species*, Darwin stated, "I should infer that probably all the organic beings which have ever lived on this earth have descended from some one primordial form, into which life was first breathed."[38] According to Darwin, the unbroken chain of life extended back millions of years, and artifacts of prehistoric man presumably represented man's ancestral roots.

Whereas Darwin claimed a connection between modern man and antiquity, the apostle Peter revealed a separation between modern man and antiquity. Peter described three separate creations: original creation, our present creation, and the future creation:

> [B]y God's word the heavens came into being and the earth was formed out of water and by water. By these waters also the world of that time was deluged and destroyed. By the same word the present heavens and earth are reserved for fire, being kept for the day of judgment and destruction of the ungodly. [I]n keeping with his promise we are looking forward to a new heaven and a new earth, where righteousness dwells. (2 Peter 3:5–7, 13)

This astonishing revelation opens a window into our past, present, and future.

First, our past: "[B]y God's word the heavens came into being and the earth was formed out of water and by water." This is God's original creation. Then, "By these waters also the world of that time was deluged and destroyed." It is critical to understand what Peter said: The *world* was deluged and destroyed. The word for "world" means, "the order of the world, the ordered universe, the ordered entirety of God's creation."[39]   In other words, it wasn't just the first Earth that was destroyed. Peter said the entirety of the first order was destroyed. Thus, the destructive waters swept across the Earth *and heavens.* (These "waters" have nothing to do with the flood of Noah. Whereas Noah's flood brought consequences confined to this current Earth, the waters spoken by Peter brought consequences that ended the first Earth and heavens.)

Peter then addressed our present: "By the same word the present heavens and earth are reserved for fire, being kept for the day of judgment and destruction of the ungodly." This present heavens and Earth are reserved for fire. Ultimately, fire will destroy this second heavens and Earth, but not until after the Day of Judgment (the Great White Throne).

Finally, Peter prophesied of our future: "[I]n keeping with his promise we are looking forward to a new heaven and a new earth, where righteousness dwells." This is the third and final creation as presented in Revelation 21 and 22.

With this understanding of Peter's revelation, this text now turns to the revelation given by John, Paul, and Moses. As God is the author, it is evident that Peter is in agreement with all three biblical writers. Additionally, Peter's New Testament revelation sheds light on the Old Testament story of creation.

In Genesis, Moses said:

> In the beginning God created the heavens and the earth. The earth was without form, and void; and darkness *was* on the face of the deep. And the Spirit of God was hovering over the face of the waters. (Gen. 1:1, 2)

"In the beginning God created the heavens and the earth." This account of creation is in agreement with Peter's account of creation: "by God's word the heavens came into being and the earth was formed out of water and by water." This is God's original creation: the first heavens and first Earth.

Then, as revealed by Peter, "by these waters also the world of that time was deluged and destroyed." This fact adds additional insight to Moses' creation account.

Firstly, the "waters" spoken by Peter that destroyed the world are the same "waters" spoken by Moses in Genesis: "The earth was without form, and void; and darkness *was* on the face of the deep. And the Spirit of God was hovering over the face of the waters." These "waters" destroyed the first order and formed the "void"—or gap in time—between the first Earth and second Earth.

Knowing the first Earth was destroyed, the first Earth *became* without form, and void of life because of the "waters." Thus, the English translation, "the earth *was* without form, and void" has to be understood as "the earth *had become* without form, and void." Supporting this position, the Hebrew word for "was" is "to become."[40]

Armed with Peter's revelation and Moses' revelation the following is clear: The first Earth—which once teemed with life—became void of it. Looking back in time, God's first Earth is, "Creation in eternity past, to which all Fossils and 'Remains' belong."[41]

Looking to the present, God's second Earth is the home for modern man.

> So God created man in his own image, in the image of God created he him; male and female created he them. And God blessed them, and God said unto them, Be fruitful, and multiply, and replenish the earth. (Gen. 1: 27, 28)

God told man to "replenish the earth." Why? Why would man replenish the Earth if it never had life prior to man's creation? In light of Peter's revelation, replenishing an empty Earth makes perfect sense.

Following the void, God reinfused life back into the planet. The apostle Paul said God created various forms of life, each having their own distinct flesh and seed: "God gives it a body as he has determined, and to each kind of seed he gives its own body. Not all flesh is the same: People have one kind of flesh, animals have another, birds another and fish another" (1 Cor.

15:38, 39). Thus, God brought forth the present order: "By the same word the present heavens and earth are reserved."

Our second order differs from the first order, and likewise, our second order will differ from the third order: the new Heaven and new Earth. When the apostle John prophesied of a "new sky (heaven) and a new earth," he referred to this present creation as "the former sky and the former earth" (Rev. 21:1). With the creation of the new Heaven and new Earth, the "former order of things" will pass away (Rev. 21:4).

(Note: When the new Earth is created it will be the third Earth and this present Earth will become the "former Earth." Some Bibles state that our current Earth is the "first Earth" (Rev. 21:1). However, this interpretation cannot be correct in light of Peter's revelation. Our current Earth is the second Earth, and thus, the Greek word is correctly translated "former" Earth, which one day will represent the "former" order of things.)

To summarize, John illuminated the present and future, and Peter illuminated the past, present, and future. Significantly, Peter's revelation about the first and second creation—and the gap between creations—is in direct contradiction to Darwin's theory of evolution, which states that modern man was not replenishing an empty Earth but was an extension of life's earliest beginnings.

With the theory of evolution diametrically opposed to creationism, the obvious question arises as to whether scientific evidence ever supported either position. Do fossils demonstrate an evolution of or a creation of a species? This issue was addressed by a biochemist named D. B. Gower. In his article titled "Scientist Rejects Evolution," Gower cited material evidence when he stated that fully developed species appeared at given points in time—all along the time continuum. Gower wrote:

> The creation account in Genesis and the theory of evolution could not be reconciled. One must be right and the other wrong. The story of the fossils agreed with the account of Genesis. In the oldest rocks we did not find a series of fossils covering the gradual changes from the most primitive creatures to developed forms, but rather in the oldest rocks developed species suddenly appeared. Between every species there was a complete absence of intermediate fossils.[42]

Fossilized evidence supports the instantaneous appearance of various creations. It does not support an ongoing evolution within a unified creation.

Even with all the research conducted in the twentieth century, a scientific link between mankind and another species never materialized. Michael Denton, an Australian molecular biologist, addressed this ongoing issue of evidence in his 1986 book, *Evolution: A*

Theory in Crisis:

> The fact is that the evidence was so patchy
> one hundred years ago that even Darwin
> himself had increasing doubts as to the
> validity of his views. The only aspect of his
> theory which has received any support over
> the past century is where it applies to micro
> evolutionary phenomena. His general theory
> that all life on earth had originated and
> evolved by a gradual successive
> accumulation of fortuitous mutations is still,
> as it was in Darwin's time, a highly
> speculative hypothesis entirely without
> factual support.[43]

Although Darwin's theory of evolution finds
support on a micro level (evolution occurring
within a given species), Darwin's general
theory—that man evolved from an entirely
different species—remains a "highly speculative
hypothesis."

Emerging evidence continues to reveal a
picture other than what Darwin painted. Late in
the twentieth century, a group of German and
American scientists extracted DNA from the
bone of a Neanderthal/Neandertal man. (Either
spelling is correct.) (Neanderthals lived between
300,000 B.C. and 30,000 B.C. in the Middle
East, Western Asia, and Europe.) The scientific
team compared Neanderthal DNA to that of
modern man, and found that the Neanderthal
sequence fell well outside the range of variation

found in humankind. Dr. Mark Stoneking, associate professor of anthropology at Penn State, stated: "These results indicate that Neandertals did not contribute mitochondrial DNA to modern humans. Neandertals are not our ancestors."[44]

How can a scientist definitively state that life within modern man is absolutely linked to other pre-existing life forms? To draw such a conclusion from existing evidence would be an unthinkable departure from the "scientific method," for in applying this approach, a valid conclusion demands unmistakable evidence linking cause and effect. Michael J. Behe, associate professor of biochemistry at Lehigh University and author of *Darwin's Black Box: The Biochemical Challenge to Evolution*, addressed the issue of causation in the following manner:

> "Evolution" implies that random mutation and natural selection powered the changes in life. The idea is that just by chance an animal was born that was slightly faster or stronger than its siblings. Its descendants inherited the change and eventually won the contest of survival over the descendants of other members of the species. Over time, repetition of the process resulted in great changes—and, indeed, wholly different animals. That's the theory. A practical difficulty, however, is that one can't test the theory from fossils.[45]

Adding to the dilemma, Darwin openly acknowledged his need to transcend classic scientific boundaries in order to produce his evolutionary conclusion. In a letter to a Harvard biology professor, Darwin wrote, "I am quite conscious that my speculations run beyond the bounds of true science."[46]

This position held by Darwin is clearly understood in light of the observation made by British scientist L. Merson Davies: "It has been estimated that no fewer than 800 phrases in the subjunctive mood (such as "Let us assume," or "We may well suppose," etc.) are to be found between the covers of Darwin's *Origin of Species* alone."[47] Without question, this approach produced an unsettling effect on objectivity. As stated by Michael Denton:

> Ultimately the Darwinian theory of evolution is no more nor less than the great cosmogenic myth of the twentieth century.[48]

Ironically, although scientists and prophets disagree with Darwin's conclusions, they agree with one of his observations. Darwin observed, "when a species has vanished from the face of the earth, the same form never reappears."[49] This observation agrees with creation theory. Once a species is extinct, it cannot regenerate itself.

Evolutionists contend that extinction occurs when a species evolves out of existence; when the evolutionary cycle is complete, the species simply ceases to exist. In contrast, creationists state that a species doesn't evolve out of existence, but rather dies out of existence. Extinction comes by way of the death of an entire life form. A species ceases to exist because the seed that produced that species died with it. Like the dinosaur kingdom, which went into decline some sixty-five million years ago, no extinct kingdoms of life have ever reappeared. Without seed, there is no possibility of life.

No conflict exists between creationists and Darwin's view about the regeneration of life. It is with Darwin's conclusion that the prophets, apostles, and scientific evidence disagree.

The conclusion—that modern man is the product of lower intelligence—excludes the need for the existence of higher intelligence. Darwinian theorists need irrefutable evidence in order to believe in a supernatural creator. The irony is that the same theorists discard this standard upon accepting the theory of evolution as fact.

If fossilized evidence supports creation theory, why not embrace the current facts and the possibility of supernatural intelligence? Could it be that an entire dimension of life cannot be measured in a laboratory? Can love be analyzed in a test tube? No, but no one doubts its existence. Can we be sure that life is confined to the boundaries of human intellect? Perhaps it is profoundly unscientific to conclude that nothing exists outside of our own sphere of understanding. What if the prophets and apostles are right about the existence of another intelligence? Then the riddle of the universe is no longer shrouded in mystery.

As stated in the biblical writings, God's word "fueled" the birth of the cosmos (the ordered universe). The prophets and apostles speak of creation as an ongoing materialization of organized matter.

In contrast, existing theory speaks of an explosion of dispersing matter. Known as the "Big Bang," the theory assumes that a "cosmic egg" exploded, shooting various materials throughout the dark expanse of space. "One second, according to theory, there was nothingness. The next, our cosmos sprang into existence."[50]

Recent astronomical findings, however, have called into question this position. In the article titled "Big Bang Theory under Fire," William C. Mitchel wrote: "[E]vidence against the BB [Big Bang] has been building to the point where the world may soon start to doubt it."[51]

Until recently, astronomers generally believed that the cosmic expansion was gradually slowing down as a result of the gravitational attraction exerted within the known universe. This logic was not lost on the Big Bang model, which assumed that a cosmic blast would ultimately produce a decelerating cosmic expansion, the obvious assumption being that an explosion that took place billions of years ago would be slowing down by now.

The problem with this assumption is that the cosmos is engaged in the opposite direction. Astronomers have discovered "that some mysterious force [is] acting against the pull of gravity, causing galaxies to fly away from each other at ever greater speeds. In one sense, the idea is not completely new. Einstein included such an 'anti-gravity' effect in his theory of general relativity."[52]   Yet, as the twentieth century drew to a close, "no one expected that the effect would turn out to be real."[53]   Recent astronomical findings reveal that invisible energy is driving the galactic expansion, "and it seems likely now that this expansion will continue indefinitely."[54]

This finding has given birth to a "harrowing new theory about the death of the universe [which] paints a picture of 'phantom energy' ripping apart galaxies, stars, planets and eventually every speck of matter in a fantastical end to time."[55]   Robert Caldwell of Dartmouth University, lead author of this theory, explains that it is one possible outcome for solid astronomical observations made in the late 1990s. (It wasn't long ago that many cosmologists believed the universe might reverse course, and that normal gravity would win, causing everything to collapse inward.)

The energy that is driving the galactic expansion is referred to as "dark energy." What is dark energy? At this time, scientists cannot explain it; they can only detect it.

Adding to this cosmic puzzle, astronomers

have discovered the presence of unseen matter in space. Called "dark matter," this material represents another unseen force in the cosmos, and some forms of this material are theorized to be radically different from matter found on Earth.

Ordinary matter on this planet is composed of protons, neutrons, and electrons, otherwise known collectively as atoms. Although the newly discovered dark matter exhibits this type of structure, more exotic forms of the material are thought to be composed of a "sea of massive particles."[56]

The discovery of dark matter is considered to be "groundbreaking." This unseen matter exerts a gravitational pull on celestial objects, and "by measuring these mysterious effects of gravity, researchers determine how much extra gravity is present, and therefore how much extra mass, or dark matter, must exist."[57]

Kim Griest, a physicist at the University of California, has worked since the mid-1990s on a project called "microlensing." It is a process used to "infer the presence of unseen objects by noting how more distant light is bent as it travels past the hidden object."[58] With this system came the discovery of dark matter.

More than three dozen elusive white dwarf stars have been found in a halo of objects surrounding our galaxy, marking the first direct evidence for previously unseen "dark matter" and lending support to a widely held theory that there is much more to the universe than meets the eye.[59] "[C]urrent theories can't cope" with such a finding and it would "trigger a revolution" in ideas about how galaxies and stars form and evolve.[60]

The coming revolution in thinking about the origin of the universe and its continuing expansion is the direct result of unseen forces at work in the cosmos. Traditional theories find no comfort in this new astronomical evidence. Could it be that the cosmic expansion is not slowing down because there never was an explosion to begin with?

As William Mitchel reminded all of us, "It is all but forgotten that the BB [Big Bang] is not fact, but an unproven theory."[61] Not only is it unproven, the theory has already gone bust in the minds of modern scientific thinkers. As cited by Eric J. Lerner in his book, *The Big Bang Never Happened,* "in the past few years, observation after observation has contradicted the predictions of this theory."[62]

Recent astronomical findings are overturning traditional thinking about the cosmos and, simultaneously, the collected data point to huge gaps in our understanding. As stated by astronomer Richard Ellis of Caltech, "I find it very worrying that you have a universe where there are three constituents, of which only one [i.e., ordinary matter] is really physically understood."[63]

If astronomers acknowledge the presence of

energy and matter that exceeds our current understanding, then what else in the cosmos exceeds our understanding? If life exists among ordinary visible matter, does life exist among invisible matter? Why couldn't there be unseen intelligence that exists in another world in another life form? Can spirit beings and angels also exist?

If unseen forces are at work throughout the galaxies, are unseen forces also at work upon the Earth? Could it be that recent astronomical evidence is just beginning to reveal the fingerprints of a higher intelligence?

If unknown energy exceeds the gravitational attraction of galaxies, is it possible the source of the energy is that which also created the galaxies, the Creator?

If science has provided a new understanding of the cosmos, it cannot help altering the way we think about the origin of the universe, man, and his destiny. Truly, there is more to the universe than can be detected by normal empirical means. If our long-held assumptions about creation are incorrect, then where is the human mind to turn?

At the start of the twenty-first century, we should ask: Is it more logical to conclude that the prophets and apostles were divinely inspired? Or were they just trying to explain our world with their own understanding of it? It cannot be both. The biblical writings either speak of our past, present, and future or they do not. Pursuing this thought, I would like to turn your attention to the archaeological community as it pertains to the Middle East.

In the mid-nineteenth century, archaeological explorers were drawn to the Holy Land in search of the past. Their collective efforts focused on one central thought: to determine the accuracy of history chronicled in the Bible. After more than one hundred fifty years of searching, the results obtained by the archaeological community have been staggering. David Rohl, author of *A Test of Time*, states: "Without initially starting out to discover the historical Bible, I have come to the conclusion that much of the Old Testament contains real history."[64]

In essence, archaeologists have discovered corroborating evidence from extra-biblical sources, and on numerous occasions have demonstrated the reliability and plausibility of what was recorded thousands of years ago. Through ancient artifacts, scientists have given the modern world a glimpse into life that once was, revealing a voice that speaks to us from the past.

With regard to the authenticity of the biblical texts, extraordinary evidence surfaced in the mid-twentieth century. The Dead Sea Scrolls, which have been referred to by scholars as the greatest manuscript discovery of modern times, were discovered between 1947 and 1956 in caves along the shore of the Dead Sea. Among over eight hundred scrolls are the oldest known versions of all but one of the books of the Old

Testament. The rest offer an intriguing picture of life in the Holy Land at the time Jesus taught in Jerusalem.

The conclusion drawn by scholars is that the biblical texts found in the scrolls are in substantial agreement with translations of the Old Testament used today. Significant among the scrolls is a virtually intact copy of Isaiah; it predates the earliest known Isaiah manuscript by one thousand years.

Scientists have concluded that the Dead Sea Scrolls were transcribed between the years 200 B.C. and 68 A.D. (This conclusion is based on carbon 14 dating: a highly accurate process that measures the decay of carbon 14, which is a radioactive element that erodes at a constant rate over time.) Of additional importance, the scientific community revealed that the critical biblical manuscripts were dated prior to 100 B.C. This is worth noting because the biblical scrolls found in the twentieth century provided documentation that the Messianic prophecies (about the first coming of Christ) were written before the dawn of the first century.

The apostles who wrote to us during the first century—speaking about the fulfillment of these Messianic prophecies—revealed that God communicated divine prophecy to Earth by way of the man called Jesus.

The record that Jesus lived in the Holy Land is not disputed. Reputable historians agree that the story of this prophet was not just a legend; historical writings support the claims made about Him. Hence, it is not a matter of whether Jesus lived, but rather, was He the Son of God?

Some people dismiss Jesus Christ as a fake hero. Yet millions hail Him as Savior and Lord. Whatever people think of Him, nobody can deny that His life represented a pivotal point in human history. His influence on humanity is unquestioned. Historian Phillip Schaff described the overwhelming influence of Christ's life:

> This Jesus of Nazareth, without money and arms, conquered more millions than Alexander, Caesar and Napoleon; without science he shed more light on things human and divine than all philosophers and scholars combined; without the eloquence of schools, he spoke such words of life as were never spoken before or since, and produced effects which lie beyond the reach of orator or poet; without writing a single line, he set more pens in motion, and furnished themes for more sermons, orations, discussions, learned volumes, works of art, and songs of praise than the whole army of great men of ancient and modern times.[65]

To conclude, scientific evidence has given us reason to believe the biblical account of creation is not simply the product of fertile and imaginative minds. If the biblical account of creation is true, then what of the biblical accounts of prophecy? Jesus Christ would have us understand this: It is not a matter of whether

Earth has been informed of its future but a matter of whether its population heeds it.

Astronomers and archeologists have given us an entirely new way of looking at the Earth and the universe. Perhaps we all owe it to ourselves to be more open to another way of knowing.

The 40th Psalm

A Psalm of David

I waited patiently for the Lord;
And He inclined to me,
And heard my cry.
He also brought me up out of a horrible pit,
Out of the miry clay,
And set my feet upon a rock,
And established my steps.

He has put a new song in my mouth
Praise to our God;
Many will see *it* and fear,
And will trust in the Lord.

Blessed *is* that man who makes the Lord his
trust,
And does not respect the proud, nor such as turn
aside to lies.
Many, O Lord my God, *are* Your wonderful
works
Which You have done;
And Your thoughts toward us
Cannot be recounted to You in order;
If I would declare and speak *of them,*
They are more than can be numbered.

Sacrifice and offering You did not desire;
My ears You have opened.
Burnt offering and sin offering You did not
require.
Then I said, "Behold, I come;
In the scroll of the book *it is* written of me.
I delight to do Your will, O my God,
And Your law *is* within my heart."

I have proclaimed the good news of
righteousness
In the great assembly;
Indeed, I do not restrain my lips,
O Lord, You Yourself know.
I have not hidden Your righteousness within my
heart;
I have declared Your faithfulness and Your
salvation;
I have not concealed Your lovingkindness and
Your truth
From the great assembly.

Do not withhold Your tender mercies from me,
O Lord;
Let Your loving kindness and Your truth
continually preserve me.
For innumerable evils have surrounded me;
My iniquities have overtaken me, so that I am
not able to look up;
They are more than the hairs of my head;
Therefore my heart fails me.

Be pleased, O Lord, to deliver me;
O Lord, make haste to help me!
Let them be ashamed and brought to mutual
confusion
Who seek to destroy my life;
Let them be driven backward and brought to
dishonor
Who wish me evil.
Let them be confounded because of their shame,
Who say to me, "Aha, aha!"

Let all those who seek You rejoice and be glad in
You;
Let such as love Your salvation say continually,
"The Lord be magnified!"

But I *am* poor and needy;
Yet the Lord thinks upon me.
You *are* my help and my deliverer;
Do not delay, O my God.

The following commentary on the 40th
Psalm is taken from *Selections from the Book of
Psalms*:

At age 12, I was a fan of David. He felt
familiar like a pop star could feel familiar.
The words of the psalms were poetic as they
were religious and he was a star. Years ago,
we were still looking for a song to close our
third album, *War*. We thought about the
psalms. "Psalm 40" is interesting in that it
suggests a time in which grace will replace

karma, and love replace the very strict laws of Moses (i.e., fulfill them). I love that thought.[66]

—Bono, U2

The Photographs

The front and back cover photos, as well as the TimeLine International, Inc. logo photo, are courtesy of NASA and the Hubble Space Telescope.

Front cover photo: A String of Cosmic Pearls Surrounds an Exploding Star
http://hubblesite.org/gallery/album/entire/pr2007016w/

Back cover photo: Scattered Light from the Boomerang Nebula
http://hubblesite.org/gallery/album/heritage/pr2005025a/

TimeLine International, Inc. logo photo: Spiral Galaxy NGC 4622
http://heritage.stsci.edu/2002/03/index.html

Endnotes

[1] John 8:32.

[2] Matt. 6:20.

[3] 2 Tim. 3:16.

[4] Rev. 3:22.

[5] Bob Dylan, Saved, (New York, NY: Columbia Records, June 1980).

[6] AARP The Magazine, (February/March, 2015), p. 27.

[7] E. W. Bullinger, A Critical Lexicon and Concordance to the English and Greek New Testament, (Grand Rapids, MI: Zondervan Publishing House, 1995), p. 661.

[8] Ibid., 469.

[9] Ibid., 362.

[10] James Strong, Abingdon's Strong's Exhaustive Concordance of the Bible, Hebrew and Chaldee Dictionary, (Nashville, TN: Abingdon, 1981), p. 80.

[11] Ibid., 112.

[12] E. W. Bullinger, A Critical Lexicon and Concordance to the English and Greek New Testament, p. 805.

[13] James Strong, Abington's Strong's Exhaustive Concordance of the Bible, Hebrew and Chaldee Dictionary, p. 819.

[14] "Rapture." Available at: https://en.wikipedia.org/wiki/Rapture. Retrieval date: January 30, 2016.

[15] E. W. Bullinger, A Critical Lexicon and Concordance to the English and Greek New Testament, p. 428.

[16] Ibid., 103.

[17] In the Psalms, there is a prayer. The Psalmist asks that the workers of iniquity (evil) would be blotted out of the book of life and not be found with the righteous.

Add iniquity unto their iniquity; And let them not come into thy righteousness. Let them be blotted out of the book of life, And not be written with the righteous. (Ps. 69:27, 28)

The prayer is about those who engage in unrighteous works being blotted out of the book of life. Thus, this reference to the book of life in the Old Testament provides the foundation for understanding the nature of this book: It is about works. Without the blood of Lamb, one can be blotted out by unrighteous works. The erroneous belief that members of an eternal kingdom can be blotted out of the book of life, resulting in loss of eternal life, is tragic. This belief cannot stand the test of the Scriptures. The King's kingdom remains eternally in the book of life, and likewise in the Lamb's book of life.

[18] E. W. Bullinger, A Critical Lexicon and Concordance to the English and Greek New Testament, p. 370.

[19] James Strong, Abingdon's Strong's Exhaustive Concordance of the Bible, Hebrew and Chaldee Dictionary, p. 63.

[20] Arthur A. Rouner, Jr., Receiving the Spirit at the Old First Church, (New York,: The Pilgrim Press, 1982), p. 22.

[21] Ibid., 23.

[22] Ibid.

[23] Ibid.

[24] Preface vii.

[25] E. W. Bullinger, A Critical Lexicon and Concordance to the English and Greek New Testament, p. 626.

[26] "The day of the Lord" (spoken of in the Old and New Testaments) has numerous implications, but all refer to

the Lord's intervention: Isa. 2:12, 13, 34; 2:12; 13:6, 9; 34:8; Jer. 46:10; Ezek. 13:5; 30:3; Joel 1:15; 2:1; 3:14; Amos 5:20; Ob. 1:15; Zeph. 1:7, 8, 14, 18; 2:2, 3; Zech. 14:1; Acts 2:20; 1 Thess. 5:2; 1 Peter 3:10.

[27] E. W. Bullinger, A Critical Lexicon and Concordance to the English and Greek New Testament, p. 202.

[28] "[T]he Shofar [trumpet] attained its chief and lasting religious importance in connection with the New Year's festival (Rosh HaShanah), celebrated on the 1st of Tishri (Lev. 23:24; Num. 29:1)." The Universal Jewish Encyclopedia, (The Universal Jewish Encyclopedia, Inc., New York, 1942), 514.

[29] The Son of God marked a gap in time (between His first and second coming to Israel) within which the mystery of the church would flourish when He quoted Isaiah:

He [Jesus] went to Nazareth, where he had been brought up, and on the Sabbath day he went into the synagogue, as was his custom. He stood up to read, and the scroll of the prophet Isaiah was handed to him. Unrolling it, he found the place where it was written:

"The Spirit of the Lord is on me, because he has anointed me to proclaim good news to the poor. He has sent me to proclaim freedom for the prisoners and recovery of sight for the blind, to set the oppressed free, to proclaim the year of the Lord's favor." Then he rolled up the scroll, gave it back to the attendant and sat down. The eyes of everyone in the synagogue were fastened on him. He began by saying to them, "Today this scripture is fulfilled in your hearing." (Luke 4:16–21)

When Jesus read this from the scroll of Isaiah, he closed the scroll after he read, "to proclaim the year of the Lord's favor." For, that is the prophecy He would fulfill. Thus, He said to the crowd: "Today this scripture is fulfilled in your hearing."

Now, look at Isaiah's prophecy. Jesus' quote is capitalized.

THE SPIRIT OF THE SOVEREIGN LORD IS ON ME, BECAUSE THE LORD HAS ANOINTED ME TO PREACH GOOD NEWS TO THE POOR. HE HAS SENT ME TO BIND UP THE BROKENHEARTED, TO PROCLAIM FREEDOM FOR THE CAPTIVES AND RELEASE FROM DARKNESS FOR THE PRISONERS, TO PROCLAIM THE YEAR OF THE LORD'S FAVOR and the day of vengeance of our God. (Isa. 61:1, 2)

Jesus never read, "and the day of vengeance of our God," for that time would come at a future point in time: His second coming to Israel. He stopped after reading, "the year of the Lord's favor," because it applied to His day and time, His first coming to Israel. Herein, Christ marked the gap the time: His first coming to Israel would fulfill the first part of Isaiah's prophecy, and His second coming to Israel would fulfill the second part. The mystery would unfold between these two points in time.

Peter's prophecy on Pentecost revealed the mystery hidden in Joel's prophecy (Joel 2:28–32a). Thus, Peter presented the gap in time, the mystery. Peter never read the rest of Joel's prophecy, "for on Mount Zion and in Jerusalem there will be deliverance, as the Lord has said, even among the survivors whom the Lord calls" (Joel 2:32b). He didn't read it because that applied to a future time: the second coming of Christ to save Israel, as did the rest of Joel's prophecy (Joel 3:1–17). The opening section of Joel's prophecy (Acts 2:17) referred to the first coming of Christ and the fulfillment of the Holy Spirit being poured out.

[30] The NIV Study Bible, (Grand Rapids, Mich.: Zondervan Publishing House, 1995), p. 1941.

[31] New Illustrated Bible Dictionary, (Nashville, Tenn.: Thomas Nelson Publishers, 1995), p. 818.

32 E. W. Bullinger, A Critical Lexicon and Concordance to the English and Greek New Testament, p. 644.

33 In 2 Thessalonians, the Apocalypse is at the heart of Paul's prophecy, and he states the church need not fear it.

Seeing it is a righteous thing with God to recompense tribulation to them that trouble you; And to you who are troubled rest with us, when the Lord Jesus shall be revealed from heaven with his mighty angels, In flaming fire taking vengeance on them that know not God, and that obey not the gospel of our Lord Jesus Christ: Who shall be punished with everlasting destruction from the presence of the Lord, and from the glory of his power; When he shall come to be glorified in his saints, and to be admired in all them that believe (because our testimony among you was believed) in that day. (2 Thess. 1:6–10)

This is the Apocalypse, when Christ returns from Heaven with His armies to defeat the Antichrist and his armies. This long-prophesied event correlates with Revelation 19 and Matthew 24. The Rapture will come to pass years before, which correlates with Revelation 6 and 7 and 1 Thessalonians 4 and 5.

This straightforward chronology, first revealed by Paul, was lost on some in the church during the first century. Therefore, in the church, an erroneous belief circulated: The Rapture had already taken place and the Apocalypse was "at hand."

Paul referenced this error in his letter to Timothy. Paul spoke of those "who have departed from the truth. They say that the resurrection has already taken place, and they destroy the faith of some" (2 Tim. 2:18). This error—believing the resurrection of the Rapture had already taken place—caused much grief among those who heard this dogma, and thus, Paul had to address it. Paul's prophecy continued:

Now we beseech you, brethren, by the coming of our

Lord Jesus Christ, and by our gathering together unto him, That ye be not soon shaken in mind, or be troubled, neither by spirit, nor by word, nor by letter as from us, as that the day of Christ is at hand. (2 Thess. 2:1, 2)

In the first-century church, some members erroneously believed the Apocalypse was "at hand" (imminent), and that the Rapture had already taken place. To combat this error, Paul beseeched the church: In light of the clear doctrine of the "gathering together" (the Rapture), and the clear doctrine of being saved from the wrath to come by the Rapture, do not to give heed to the false belief that the church would be present on Earth during the wrath, when the Apocalypse would be imminent. Then, Paul explained why.

Let no man deceive you by any means: for that day [the day of Christ, the Apocalypse] shall not come, except there come a falling away first, and that man of sin [the Antichrist] be revealed, the son of perdition. (2 Thess. 2:3)

Paul had already told those in Thessalonica this: The Apocalypse is not at hand (present) because that day will not come until the Earth is filled with unrighteous, which is the "falling away" (Greek: Apostasy, E. W. Bullinger, A Critical Lexicon and Concordance to the English and Greek New Testament, p. 274).

The apostasy will come to pass after the Rapture during the time of wrath, when men shall turn their hearts to worship the Antichrist. Paul had already explained in 1 Thessalonians that the church is saved from the wrath to come.

If the church is saved from the wrath and thus not present for the apostasy, it is impossible for the church to be present during the Apocalypse. Paul beseeched them in light of the comfort and hope of the gathering of the Rapture not to give heed to the belief the church would be present on Earth during the Apocalypse. Hence, he exhorted the church not to be "shaken."

When Paul described the Apocalypse, he did so by saying "the day of Christ," not the "day of the Lord." (The Greek text supports the use of "Christ" in 2 Thessalonians, for it is the word, Christos (George Ricker Barry, The Interlinear Greek-English New Testament, (Michigan,: Zondervan, 1980), p. 536).

Paul is drawing a distinction between the "day of the Lord" in 1 Thessalonians, which he used to refer to the Rapture, and "the day of Christ" in 2 Thessalonians, which he used to refer to the Apocalypse.

Paul comforted the church by saying this: God is holding back the time of the Antichrist. "And now you know what is holding him back, so that he may be revealed at the proper time (2 Thess. 2:6). John clearly revealed this "proper time" in Revelation 13.

Paul finished his prophecy in 2 Thessalonians with confirmation as to why the church need not be shaken: sanctification and the hope of glory.

But we are bound to give thanks to God always for you, brethren beloved by the Lord, because God from the beginning chose you for salvation through sanctification by the Spirit and belief in the truth, to which He called you by our gospel, for the obtaining of the glory of our Lord Jesus Christ. Therefore, brethren, stand fast and hold the traditions which you were taught, whether by word or our epistle. Now may our Lord Jesus Christ Himself, and our God and Father, who has loved us and given us everlasting consolation and good hope by grace, comfort your hearts and establish you in every good word and work. (2 Thess. 2:13–17)

[34] According to Hebrew authorities, "the last trumpet" and "the great trumpet" are not one and the same; they mark unique sounds. Yet, both "the last trumpet" and "the great trumpet" sound on the same holy day: the Feast of

Trumpets. On the Feast of Trumpets, the trumpet sounds 101 times. This number is divided as follows: 30, 30, 40, and 1.

The Great Trumpet: "[The] Ram's horn [Shofar] sounded on New Year's. A series of thirty blasts continued in quick succession is called the Great Teki'a." (The Encyclopedia of Jewish Knowledge (New York: Behrman's Jewish Book House, 1944), p. 514.)

The Last Trumpet (final, single blast): "The last Tekiah, known as Tekiah Gedolah, is prolonged as long as the breath of the officiant holds out."(The Universal Jewish Encyclopedia, (The Universal Jewish Encyclopedia, Inc., New York, 1942), p. 515.)

The great trumpet will sound following the sign of the moon turning dark, signaling the Apocalypse and gathering of Israel. The last trumpet will sound following the sign of the blood red moon, signaling the Rapture of the church. Both trumpets sound on the Feast of Trumpets, signaling deliverance.

35 D. J. Futuyma, Science on Trial: The Case for Evolution. New York: Pantheon Books, 1993, 197. Available at http://www.pathlights.com. "Scientists Speak about Evolution." Retrieval date: Dec. 17, 2001.

36 Michael Denton, Evolution: A Theory in Crisis. Chevy Chase, Md.: Adler & Adler Publishers, Inc., 1986, p. 67. Available at http://www.pathlights.com. "Scientists Speak about Evolution." Retrieval date: Dec. 17, 2001.

37 Richard Weikart, "Does Darwinism Devalue Human Life," The Human Life Review, March 1, 2004. Available at http://www.discovery.org/a/2172. Retrieval date: May 21, 2016.

38 Charles Darwin, On the Origin of Species. Chapter 14: Recapitulation and Conclusion. Available at https://sciweek.wordpress.com/2012/09/20/evolution-

this-evolution-that/ "Evolution this-evolution that." Retrieval date: May 21, 2016.

39 E. W. Bullinger, A Critical Lexicon and Concordance to the English and Greek New Testament, p. 900.

40 E.W. Bullinger, The Companion Bible (Grand Rapids, Mich.: Kregel Publications, 1990), p. 3.

41 Ibid.

42 D. B. Gower, "Scientist Rejects Evolution," Kentish Times, Dec. 11, 1975, Kent, England, p. 4. Available at http://www.pathlights.com. "Scientists Speak about Evolution." Retrieval date: Dec. 17, 2001.

43 Michael Denton, Evolution: A Theory in Crisis, p. 77.

44 "DNA Shows Neandertals Were Not Our Ancestors." EurekAlert! Available at http://www.eurekalert.org/pub_releases/1997-07/PS-DSNW-100797.php. Retrieval date: May 21, 2016.

45 Michael J. Behe, "Darwin under the Microscope," The New York Times, Oct. 29, 1996, Tuesday Final, Section A, p. 25. Available at http://www.arn.org/docs/behe/mb_dm11496.htm. Retrieval date: Dec. 17, 2001.

46 N. C. Gillespie, Charles Darwin and the Problem of Creation. Chicago: University of Chicago, 1979, p. 2. Available at http://www.pathlights.com. "Scientists Speak about Evolution." Retrieval date: Dec. 17, 2001.

47 L. Merson Davies, Modern Science, 1953, p. 7. Available at http://www.pathlights.com. "Scientists Speak about Evolution." Retrieval date: Dec. 17, 2001.

48 Michael Denton, Evolution: A Theory in Crisis, p. 358.

49 John Patrick Michael Murphy, "Charles Darwin," 1999. Available at http://www.infidels.org/library/modern/john_murphy/charlesdarwin.html. Retrieval date: Dec. 17, 2001.

50 Andrew Chalkin, "Are There Other Universes?" Feb. 5, 2002. Available at http://www.space.com. Retrieval date: Feb. 5, 2002.

51 William C. Mitchel, "Big Bang Theory under Fire," Physics Essays (vol. 10, no. 2), June 1997. Available at http://nowscape.com/big-ban2.htm. Retrieval date: Feb. 4, 2002.

52 Andrew Chalkin, "Dark Energy: Astronomers Still 'Clueless' about Mystery Force Pushing Galaxies Apart," January 15, 2002. Available at http://www.space.com. Retrieval date: Feb. 4, 2002.

53 Ibid.

54 Ibid.

55 Robert Roy Britt, "The Big Rip: New Theory Ends Universe by Shredding Everything," March 6, 2003. Available at http://www.space.com. Retrieval date: March 6, 2003.

56 Robert Roy Britt, "'Groundbreaking' Discovery: First Observation of Dark Matter," March 22, 2001. Available at http://www.space.com. Retrieval date: Jan. 23, 2002.

57 Robert Roy Britt, "Understanding Dark Matter and Light Energy," Jan. 5, 2001. Available at http://www.space.com. Retrieval date: Jan. 23, 2002.

58 Robert Roy Britt, "'Groundbreaking' Discovery: First Observation of Dark Matter."

59 Ibid.

60 Ibid.

61 Mitchel, "Big Bang Theory under Fire."

62 Eric Lerner, The Big Bang Never Happened. (New York: Vintage Books, 1992), p. 4.

63 Andrew Chalkin, "Dark Energy: Astronomers Still 'Clueless' about Mystery Force Pushing Galaxies Apart."

64 David Rohl, A Test of Time. Available at

http://www.freerepublic.com/focus/f-news/725672/posts. "A New Chronology," John Fulton. Retrieval date: May 21, 2016.

[65] Available at http://www.whoisJesus-really.com. Retrieval date: Jan. 20, 2002.

[66] Selections from the Book of Psalms (New York: Grove Press, 1999), p. vii.

Made in the USA
Middletown, DE
16 May 2017